PERGAMON INSTITUTE OF ENGLISH (OXFORD)

Language Teaching Methodology Series

ENGLISH BY MAGIC
A Resource Book

ENGLISH BY MAGIC
A Resource Book

Peter John Hassall

PERGAMON INSTITUTE OF ENGLISH

a member of the Pergamon Group

Oxford · New York · Toronto · Sydney · Paris · Frankfurt

U.K.	Pergamon Press Ltd., Headington Hill Hall, Oxford OX3 0BW, England
U.S.A.	Pergamon Press Inc., Maxwell House, Fairview Park, Elmsford, New York 10523, U.S.A.
CANADA	Pergamon Press Canada Ltd., Suite 104, 150 Consumers Road, Willowdale, Ontario M2J 1P9, Canada
AUSTRALIA	Pergamon Press (Aust.) Pty. Ltd., P.O. Box 544, Potts Point, N.S.W. 2011, Australia
FRANCE	Pergamon Press SARL, 24 rue des Ecoles, 75240 Paris, Cedex 05, France
FEDERAL REPUBLIC OF GERMANY	Pergamon Press GmbH, Hammerweg 6, D-6242 Kronberg-Taunus, Federal Republic of Germany

Copyright © 1985 Pergamon Press Ltd.

First edition 1985

Library of Congress Cataloging in Publication Data

Hassall, Peter John
English by magic.
(Language teaching methodology series)
Includes bibliographies.
1. Language arts (Elementary) 2. English Language—
Study and teaching (Elementary) 3. Educational games.
4. Conjuring.   I. Title. II. Series.
LB1576.H313   1984   372.6'044   83-25754

British Library Cataloguing in Publication Data

Hassall, Peter John
English by magic.—(Language teaching
methodology series)
1. English language—Text-books for foreign
speakers   2. Conjuring
I. Title   II. Series
428.2'4   PE1128
ISBN 0-08-030484-2

Printed in Great Britain by A. Wheaton & Co. Ltd., Exeter

For
J. E. and S.
M. D. and K.
and all the family

Contents

Properties and Positions

Vanishing

General Introduction

This book for teachers and teacher-trainers may also be used by students. It contains a selection of magic which has been organized to help people learn and enjoy English while they perform and learn about magic. Although it is based on the communicative approach to teaching and learning, those concerned with more traditional approaches should also find the ideas and materials useful.

Part One: Teach English by Magic! provides a light-hearted introduction which may help teachers to reconsider their approach to language in the classroom. It is suitable for native and non-native speakers and uses the framework provided by well-known authorities and practitioners. The section on *Rough Magic* considers that the teacher's presentation (often thought of as analogous to that of an actor in the theatre) should itself be fully exploited to serve as a stimulus for motivation. The section on *Real Magic* considers that there is value in having a Recreation Stage in the language lesson and suggests that magic might be an appropriate activity here.

Part Two: Learn English by Magic! provides an introduction to the tricks which appear in Part Three, and outlines the various classroom approaches which may accommodate the use of magic and the levels at which the tricks may be performed.

Part Three: The Tricks is a collection of magic tricks presented in units, which can be used by teachers and students. Notes are provided for each unit.

PART ONE:

Teach English By Magic!

Some Questions Answered

Why Magic?

Magic provides a communicative theme which teachers may develop when considering their approach to both language teaching and materials development. It has two distinct advantages:
1. It is novel and therefore motivates students;
2. It may be easily slotted into everyday English lessons.

Where Magic?

Magic is useful at two stages of the English lesson:
1. At the Presentation Stage (Byrne);
2. At the Recreation Stage (adapted from Davies).

What Magic?

Magic may be divided into two categories:
1. *Rough Magic* (a term borrowed from Peter Brook, the theatre director), which is useful at the Presentation Stage;
2. *Real Magic*, which is useful at the Recreation Stage.

Brook used the term *Rough Magic* to describe the clumsy presentation of the labourers (such as Bottom and Quince) when performing their play in Shakespeare's *A Midsummer Night's Dream*. A similar presentation may be used by teachers to add variety to their lessons.

Real Magic is that performed by magicians on the stage or television. This may be utilized by students, giving them the chance to 'hold the stage' and benefit from this experience.

Which Magic?

Procedures and materials should be selected to suit both particular linguistic items and the teacher's individual style. Not all techniques outlined here will be suitable for all teachers or classes, but I hope they will provide 'food for thought'.

1

Rough Magic

At the Presentation Stage

Magic is well suited to the Presentation Stage. It provides a framework involving limited lexis, structures and functions combined with an abundance of gesture which lends itself to the presentation of new linguistic items. A context is created which may also help to establish grammatical or functional words such as the articles, auxiliary verbs, prepositions, negative and comparative particles, without which little progress can be made.

The framework it provides may be considered communicative in that the audience cannot know the outcome of the Magic and so their attention is held. Non-fictional materials such as 'What's it like?' (Andrews) and 'What colour is it?' (Nicholls *et al*) help students to interpret and communicate about the world of objects around them. Magic may provide a communicative precursor to materials such as these.

W.R. Lee's Structure Game 3 'What is there in my bag today?' is an instance of a communicative activity involving participation and everyday equipment, where students are asked to guess about objects which are first hidden by the teacher. A consideration of Rough Magic will, I hope, help to generate similar activities which may be used by the teacher at the Presentation Stage.

Guidelines

Rough Magic today is perhaps best epitomized by the comedian/magician Tommy Cooper whose 'ham-fisted' presentation created a sense of fun yet maintains the fascination of magic. Artistes like Tommy Cooper may draw upon the whole gamut of Magic to develop their presentation. However, it may help the language teacher to bear in mind the following guidelines for developing Rough Magic at the Presentation Stage:

1. Unlike Conventional Stage Magic the presentation should not be overcrowded with techniques but should concentrate on one or two to make them more memorable.
2. The language should be as economical as possible and approach the silent Magic Performance, rather than use inconsequential patter as its driving force.
3. Excessive use of illusion or sleight of hand should give way to Obvious Deception. This is quite the reverse of advice given to amateur magicians 'The means by which your magic is achieved should be as unnoticeable as possible' (Reed). With Rough Magic the students know they are being 'taken-in' and can perceive changes taking place in from of them. This light-hearted approach is to be preferred as it enables the teacher to do several things:
   (a) manipulate ordinary objects without a great deal of skill;
   (b) control the linguistic presentation fully;
   (c) maintain the sense of trust between himself and the students (he is not 'taking them in' without their knowledge);
   (d) frustrate and thereby motivate the students;
   (e) add a sense of fun to the proceedings by suggesting that the teacher is an incompetent magician who is cheating – 'Teacher and student alike must be

shaken loose from their timid perfectionism if anything creative is to take place' (Stevick).

I think these guidelines make the presentation 'rough' enough. Now where does the Magic come in?

The Essence of Magic

It is the Essence of Magic which should be retained – careful attention to the props, the layout, the gestures and the silences. These together inhibit a 'barrage of utterances' which Gattegno's 'Silent Way' likens to a 'handful of stones thrown on a quiet pond – we are unable to follow the ripples from any one of them because of interference produced by the others' (Stevick). Without such a barrage, attention is concentrated on a kind of information gap which is the focus of all Magic, i.e. there is a discrepancy between what the magician knows about his performance and what the audience knows.

Rough Magic and the Information Gap

By using Rough Magic at the Presentation Stage, a dual information gap is created. First there is the linguistic gap which is part of all presentation, i.e. the teacher has selected the utterance(s) he wishes to present but, as yet, the students do not know what is to be presented nor what it will mean. So, when planning the Presentation Stage, the teacher need have no doubts about genuine communication taking place.

Second, an information gap is created as the students cannot know the outcome of the teacher's Rough Magic. This provides a real reason for them to ask questions such as 'How many are there?' or 'Where is it?'. This dual information gap between the teacher and the students should be highlighted so that the appropriate utterance(s) in English may be made more memorable. The teacher's Obvious Deception, which provides the central focus of Rough Magic Presentation, will initially fulfil this function and lead to reflection about what will happen next. Revealing the obvious deception will aid recognition of the utterance (relating to the outcome of the teacher's actions) and make it more meaningful.

Thus, Rough Magic can ensure a meaningful, memorable context for new items where suitable.

Presentation

Depending on the item, realia (props) may be borrowed from the 'audience' in order to maximize involvement; this way the students have truly invested something (a tangible object) and have cause to reflect (whether their property will be returned or not). This is shown in the typical presentation of Rough Magic which follows.

Item – 'How many pens are there?'

Response – 'There are xxxx'.

Teacher: Presentation	Students: Effect
1. Pick up waste-paper basket.	Familiar props/Vocabulary
2. Obtain pens from students.	Participation

3. Rattle pens in basket.	Inspection of situation
4. Gesture to focus attention.	Silence
5. Visibly 'secrete' a number of pens.	Obvious Deception
6. 'How many pens are there in the basket?'	Reception
7. Pause.	Reflection
8. Show pens in basket.	Deception exposed
9. Appropriate response supplied	Information gap filled

    (a) Teacher responds;
    (b) Teacher shows basket to others to guess.
        Exercise continues until response is
        appropriate and formally correct;
    (c) (Choral phase).

| 10. Basket is given to students to 'hold the stage'. | Repetition. |

This example has proved effective in demonstrating the appropriateness of 'How many pens are there?' in contrast to the common error 'How many is there?' as the students hear the pens rattle and think of more than one pen. The subsequent responses quickly progress to 'There is only one' and 'There aren't any' when appropriate.

In Rough Magic the teacher may select students as his 'confederates'. These students, being a party to further Rough Magic, can practise contradictions such as 'No there aren't (isn't)'. This can boost the self-confidence of students contradicting others of equal or greater ability. This proceeds to students correcting each other, without further Rough Magic or interruptions from the teacher, if an incorrect response is made. Thus the language is made more dynamic and purposeful than question/answer technique and yet can be fully controlled by the teacher who can assess the appropriateness of the linguistic content and level of difficulty for particular students.

Selection

The most obvious material suitable for Rough Magic Presentation is that concerning tangible objects. For the item 'Where is it?', objects can be 'Rough Magicked' all around the room – 'in the box', 'under the table' or 'behind the cupboard'. A hand placed in front of a small object will create the Obvious Deception; for a larger article a cloth draped over it will suffice. As Maley and Duff write: 'As soon as the familiar is temporarily removed from sight it becomes intriguing'.

Rough Magic also allows visuals (blackboard/overhead projector) to become less static by an adjustment to their content, e.g.

What's that?

It's a vase.

No it isn't.
It's a jug.

No it isn't.
It's a coffee pot.

or

It's a man.

No it isn't.
It's a woman.

No, it's the sun.

or

What's he doing?

He's running.

No he isn't.
He's playing football.

No he isn't.
He's running away from a dog.

Prepared Objects may be used with Rough Magic to teach colours etc. in a novel way. For example cards or toy cars may be painted in different colours and each side shown in turn:

	– 'It's orange'.
then Rough Magic	– 'No it isn't. It's green.'
then the deception is exposed	– 'No it isn't. It's green and orange.'

A bowl of strangely painted fruit and a blindfold is also a possible idea.

More conventional visual aids such as picture cue cards (Kerr) lend themselves to simple and obvious Rough Magic card tricks. (See section on card tricks.)

Real Magic (as outlined below) may occasionally be used at the Presentation Stage to keep the students guessing and alert. But it should be exposed at a later stage of the lesson as we intend to teach English and are not just simply trying to entertain and deceive.

Rough Magic should only be selected for Presentation if it makes the linguistic items more memorable and meaningful. It should also be only one course in a varied diet of ostensive techniques to prevent a one-to-one correspondence between an item and its mother-tongue equivalent.

Real Magic

The Recreation Stage

In his article 'All Protein and no Roughage makes Hamid a Constipated Student' Robin Davies argues for the introduction of Extra-Curricular Activities (such as jewelry making, pottery making, photography, drama and car maintenance) as they are conducive to general language-learning vitality. He stresses that students 'need to have experiences beyond the language-learning classroom in order to have anything to want to communicate. They must learn to enjoy using English in a natural context regardless of whether this contact is relevant to their long-term objective'.

Donn Byrne in *Teaching Oral English* also favoured students having 'opportunities to use the language themselves – to say what they want to say rather than what they are directed to say'. However, he argues from the opposite end of the spectrum – outlining the Production Stage as an integral part of the language lesson. Byrne is more concerned with the long-term language-learning objectives of the students; 'opinions and reactions may be elicited from the students', 'mistakes provide feedback for remedial teaching'. He suggests discussion, role-playing, drama and language games – activities more compatible with the conventional classroom than those described by Davies.

I would like to suggest a compromise between these two views to supplement the Production Stage with the introduction of a Recreation Stage integral to the language lesson. This could take place just before a break to let the students wind down after an intensive lesson and produce more 'natural' language or on a more regular basis – once a week (see Christopher Sion).

Emphasis would be placed on the students' involvement in Communicative Activities and only secondarily on diagnosis by the teacher towards language teaching goals. At this Recreation Stage students would be encouraged to engage in activities not normally encountered in the language classroom. Such activities may be characterized by their occurrence outside the classroom in contexts which are not solely designed to promote linguistic development (e.g. clubs and societies). The teacher may be considered less directive by allowing the students to choose what they want to do and say (they need to learn to do this). The students are given an opportunity to experiment at their own linguistic level as the constraints imposed by examinations and syllabuses are no longer present.

The students' interests and preferences are of prime importance at the Recreation Stage. It may include activities modified from the Production Stage such as:

debates where students decide the topic;
games (of all kinds) where students decide the game;
drama where students decide the theme;
Magic where students decide the trick.

All these topics are probably compatible with both Extra Curricular Activities and the Production Stage. There are many more.

The teacher would merely keep a 'weather eye' on their language performance whilst promoting the students' involvement in the Communicative Activities by organizing the class (informal group work will often cater for a variety of interests), advising students, learning from students (they are not just empty vessels), and only intervening when communication breaks down (Philip Riley).

As a Communicative Activity

At the Recreation Stage, magic provides a communicative theme outside the usual language syllabus similar to car maintenance or pottery making. However, it is also an activity which should interest and involve most students – almost everyone is fascinated by Magic, as it is, almost by definition, that which is intriguing or mysterious.

Second, Magic is communicative in that it involves performance which entails interaction between a magician and his audience. In a less structured sense this is also true of other activities, i.e. an informed person may tell another about car maintenance. However, the structured nature of Magic coupled with the great variety of tricks provides an excellent occasion for the equalizing of opportunity – students may take 'turns' to hold the stage, act as audience or learn new tricks. Most people (students or teachers) will already have one or two tricks 'up their sleeve' which they can bring to the Recreation Stage.

In linguistic terms Magic may be seen as complementing other Communicative Activities. It provides careful attention to language but not so obviously as debates; it also uses a great deal of gesture and equipment. It concentrates on the manipulation of the environment via tricks (dealing with words, codes such as numbers and words, and people) rather than the 'observation, sensitivity and imagination' developed by drama and games (Maley and Duff). Magic may also cater for students of lower linguistic ability as economy of language may be appreciated as much as rational exposition or imagination because the tricks themselves have their own characteristic personality.

I use the term Real Magic not only to contrast it with Rough Magic, but also to describe the Magic of conventional magicians on the stage or television. Real Magic in the classroom is most likely to approach that described in books on Amateur Magic – using simple equipment, very little skill and plenty of audience participation. However, I do not want to preclude an interest in the more professional Magic of the stage and television which is usually, though not always necessarily, less accessible in the classroom due to expense, secrecy and skill. A typical example of a Real Magic trick suitable for the Recreation Stage and included for comparison with Rough Magic is shown below:

'Mend the Match' (see *Learn English by Magic*, Unit G)

'Magician' (Student or Teacher)	*Audience Effect*
1. Secretly hide match in hem of handkerchief.	None – action not seen
2. Show another match 'Look at it. Is it broken?'	Inspection of situation
3. 'Please put the match on the handkerchief.'	Participation
4. Fold the handkerchief but hold the hidden match.	Sleight of hand
5. 'Now break the match.'	Participation
6. 'Are you sure its broken? Feel it.'	Real deception
7. Slowly open the handkerchief.	Reflection
8. 'No, you're wrong. It isn't broken.'	Illusion
9. 'Look, I've mended it.'	Frustration
10. Repeat with new match.	Reinforcement

A wealth of authentic written material is available for tricks such as the one above, much of which has already been simplified for amateurs. Students should be encouraged to decide what to study themselves so that their own preferences may be catered for (this would also allow discussion). They may find themselves confronted with both easy and difficult material. Because of this, there is no necessity for careful structural grading – although an awareness of level of difficulty and effectiveness of a trick may help the teacher to advise how best a trick might be tackled.

Students should be made aware of all the possible sources of magic; reading (books, periodicals, etc.), watching (television or shows) or talking to others. They can usefully be encouraged to help explain new tricks to less-able students (both linguistically or because they are inhibited etc.) or write out their own (ones they know, have found or invented) for others – this is a much more realistic communicative activity than explaining how to make a cup of tea or change a plug which are subjects often chosen.

Instruction writing and instruction following are the two principal activities implied by Magic. This may be analagous to the Asher Method of Total Physical Response where students learn by physically performing actions based first on commands of the teacher and then by commands of other students. Students may also be encouraged to personalize tricks – more complex tricks could be adapted to make them more suitable for their own personality and audience and vice versa. Tricks may also be combined to create new ones as there seems to be a limited number of principles on which magic is based.

As well as adapting, writing and explaining tricks, a student may also choose to perform one. This is the culmination of the Communicative Activity: 'the final stage is not reached until the class is re-formed and the students are given the opportunity to show or discuss what they have achieved' (Byrne). Performance allows students to contextualize their limited lexical, functional and structural competence into activities grounded in the real world using gesture to compensate for any linguistic inadequacies. A glance at the example of real magic outlined above ('Mend the Match') will show that many useful lexical items (show, put, fold, wrong), structural items (I've mended it) and functional items (particularly asking people to do things e.g. 'Now break the match!') may arise. Many of these items do not appear in conventional textbooks, yet often facilitate everyday communication. They may be explained with the help of gesture. Students respond, but not necessarily verbally, to such help and this enables them to build up (passive) vocabularies. As well as providing an opportunity for production as students take turns to hold the stage, there is the chance for students to develop receptive skills when they are in the audience.

Student tasks prior to performance are shown below:

1. Select a trick (possible negotiation with the teacher or colleagues);
2. Work out what the trick entails (both linguistically and practically);
3. Adapt the trick for own personality and audience (to avoid creating mere language-like behaviour);
4. Practise the trick with someone else to watch and assist;
5. Prepare for performance – assemble equipment, memorize adaptation and dispense with written materials;
6. Perform the trick (to outsiders if possible – e.g. families or other classes – to maximize motivation and preliminary involvement).

At each stage the teacher's role is to informally assist whenever necessary, i.e. whenever communication breaks down. Teachers are also admirably placed to advise students on presentation as this is a requirement of their job. The teacher may initiate an interest in magic either by practical demonstration of a trick or discussion of materials to 'provide a model of target language behaviour' (Wilkins). His responsibility then is to organize research, adaptation, practice and performance and to encourage student involvement. The students themselves must be allowed to decide whether to perform or not perform.

Conclusion

Wilkins interprets the 'essential' truth of the behaviourist view 'we learn what we do' thus – 'We learn something roughly in proportion to the degree of experience that we have of it'. I hope the Real Magic will make up for some of the inadequacies of classroom language (e.g. the danger of 'structure speech' coined by Daikin), by providing Communicative Activities which may be compared to language use in the street where 'the reward for success and punishment for failure is enormous. No civilized teacher can compete'.

Bibliography

Andrews, John, *Say what You Mean in English, Book 1*, Thomas Nelson, 1975.

Asher, James, J., 'Physical Activity as a Continuous and Integral Part of Learning' in *Learning Another Language through Actions: the Complete Teacher's Guidebook*, Sky Oak Productions, 1977.

Brook, Peter, *1970 Production of 'A Midsummer Night's Dream'* (Shakespeare) in BBC TV *Review* programme 1971, Open University Drama course A307.

Byrne, Donn, *Teaching Oral English*, Longman, 1976.

Daikin, Julian, *The Language Laboratory and Language Learning*, Longman, 1971.

Davis, Robin, 'All Protein and no Roughage makes Hamid a Constipated Student' in Holden, Susan (*ed.*) *English for Specific Purposes*, Modern English Publications, 1977.

Gattegno, Caleb, 'The Silent Way' in *The Common Sense of Teaching Foreign Languages*, Educational Solutions, 1976.

Haskell, John F., 'An Eclectic Method?' *TESOL Newsletter*, April 1978.

Kerr, J.Y.K., 'Picture Cue Cards for Pair or Group Work' in Holden, Susan (*ed.*) *Visual Aids for Classroom Interaction*, Modern English Publications, 1978.

Lee, W.R., *Language Teaching Games and Contests*, 2nd edn, Oxford University Press, 1979.

Maley, Alan and Duff, Alan, *Drama Techniques in Language Learning*, Cambridge University Press, 1978.

Nicholls, Sandra, O'Shea, Patrick and Yeadon, Tony, *English Alive Book 1*, Edward Arnold, 1977.

Reed, Graham, *Magic for Every Occasion*, Kaye & Wood, 1978.

Revell, Jane, *Teaching Techniques for Communicative English*, Macmillan, 1979.

Riley, Philip, 'When Communication Breaks Down: Levels of Coherence in Discourse' *Applied Linguistics*, Autumn 1980, Oxford University Press.

Sion, Christopher, 'Just the Thing for Friday Afternoons: Limericks' *Modern English Teacher*, September 1978.

Spolsky, Bernard, 'The Comparative Study of First and Second Language Acquisition' in Eckman, F.R. and Hastings, A.J. (*eds*) *Studies in First and Second Language Acquisition*, Newbury House, 1979.

Wilkins, D.A., *Linguistics in Language Teaching*, Edward Arnold, 1972.

Wilkins, D.A., *Second-language Learning and Teaching*, Edward Arnold, 1974.

PART TWO:

Learn English by Magic!

'There is a vast difference between telling
how a trick is done and teaching how to do it'
Angelo Lewis (*c*. 1875)

Introduction

The tricks in Part Three provide activities based on the Communicative Approach –
they may be used on a regular basis or as a stand-by (fillers for unexpected lessons and
unplanned time). There are some old tricks and new tricks, chosen because they are
all relatively 'foolproof' and may be performed using simple equipment and very little
skill in the classroom. Some of the tricks may be thought of as more suitable for students studying English for Special Purposes (ESP) courses (e.g. engineering or business) but all of them may be used in a general course of English as a Foreign Language
to help students enjoy using English and provide an opportunity for language enrich-
ment.

Often students of English (adults are no exception) reach a plateau where they can
function reasonably well in English and 'get by' with their knowledge of the world –
they can change plugs, make tea and even operate machines if told how. Their
language, however, reaches an impasse as not enough material which is challenging to
both their understanding and linguistic production is given to them. Communicative
Activities such as Magic may provide such a challenge – because it relies on performance it does not allow students to 'get-by' but ensures they are stretched in both
interpretative and productive linguistic roles.

Everyone usually knows one or two tricks in their native-tongue. Yet Magic may very
well be culture specific (as jokes) and so provide cross-cultural comparison. It is hoped
that these materials will enhance motivation and produce a great number of practice
situations in which students and teachers together will become involved to resolve
practical linguistic problems.

The Materials

The tricks have been adapted from books on Magic, many of which can be found in
libraries throughout the world. Such books have already been simplified to be used by
Amateur Magicians and English children. The materials here have been further simplified by deleting excessive use of colloquialisms and a heavy style, which have been
used to make the tricks more approachable yet mysterious but are not readily understood by non-native speakers. It is hoped that this simplification will facilitate involvement in Magic in the classroom, rather than other activities such as dictionary work.
However, this is only the beginning, and further research using Amateur Magic books
or other sources are given in the *Tasks for Students*. Students should also be encouraged to adapt the tricks for their own personalities and audiences, leaving the text
behind; this will probably entail repetition and additional explanation. The illus-

11

trations and the headings also ensure repetition which makes the language more redundant (easier to follow) than tricks found in conventional books on Magic.

The tricks are not rigorously graded in structural terms as my intention was to ensure sufficient material to provide extensive practice and at the same time challenge the students both receptively and productively. Instead tricks have been grouped together to lead to a better understanding of some of the principles underlying Magic (as I see them) so that students may introduce their own tricks to the classroom and perhaps invent new ones as well.

The tricks appear in sections under the following headings:

Section One: Dealing with Objects
Section Two: Dealing with Codes (Numbers and Words)
Section Three: Dealing with People.

Engineering students may find most relevance in Sections One and Two, Business students in sections Two and Three. However nothing rigid is implied and freedom of choice is to be encouraged; choosing tricks from a different section each time will ensure that the spectators do not become bored or see through the tricks too easily but are always confronted with something new.

Worksheets and Texts

The Worksheets have been designed primarily to develop productive linguistic skills. When they are used by students the suggested framework should be seen as a scenario, or jumping-off point of what to do and say, to develop their own presentation i.e. checking people know what the objects are and what they are being asked to do by using gesture and tone of voice (usually the sphere of the teacher) to get the trick across. The teacher should intervene to help the students develop what they want to do and say rather than letting them stick rigidly to the Worksheets. Thus inhibited or less-able students may have to rely more on gesture, whereas advanced students may be encouraged to weave stories round the tricks and ensure maximum participation. Worksheets should be adapted and practised prior to performance and any interpretative or production problems checked with the teacher and/or classmates.

The Texts which follow the Worksheets are less explicit and necessitate more development by the teacher or students as no suggestions on Presentation are given. Such material could provide a measure of student comprehension and performance by observing how effectively a student performs a trick. However this is not what is intended – with Communicative Activities (as have been discussed so far) the teacher should assist students when they have linguistic problems, advise them how to make their Presentation more effective and organize the classroom to produce an atmosphere conducive to Performance.

Classroom Organization

The teacher has often been called an organizer of learning. There are many ways of using Communicative-based material such as Magic – not all of which result in Communicative Activities as outlined above. The Approach which is chosen is dependent on the type of classroom environment in which it is used. The suggestions outlined below perhaps say more about the environment than the Magic. However, I do not propose to underestimate any one of them as I feel it is the teacher's responsibility to organize a variety of learning experiences to suit his learners' personalities and their needs at any one time.

1. Very Formal Approach – Teacher-controlled Classwork

Magic may be inappropriate in the classroom – resort to Extra-curricular Activities such as a magic club. Alternatively the materials could be used as reading comprehension passages (perhaps as a stand-by) – students encouraged to perform them at a later date outside the classroom, e.g. at home.

2. Formal Approach – Teacher-directed Classwork towards Linguistic Goals (Practice)

The teacher chooses a trick to practise functional or structural items already met. Following classwork to iron-out any linguistic problems, students may be divided into pairs for practice and performance.

3. Informal Approach – Teacher-directed Groupwork towards Linguistic/Personality Goals

The teacher chooses tricks for particular groups of students to help remedy problems he has observed. Thus tricks may be chosen to elucidate particular linguistic problems – tricks involving assistants given to mixed-ability groups to develop, or tricks given to particular groups to suit their personalities and/or interests (e.g. extrovert/introvert, etc.). Groups of five or six work well as the students (a) can help each other; (b) have someone to practise the trick with; (c) have ample supply of assistants.
The class may come together to watch students who have practised the trick effectively in their groups, or alternatively new groups may be formed, using one student from each of the original groups, so that an audience is created for each student to perform his trick – maximizing involvement of both the performers and audience as each student takes a turn.

4. Very Informal Approach – Student-centred Groupwork or Individual Tasks

This is the realm of the Communicative Recreation Stage (outlined in *Real Magic*). Students help to choose their own groups and decide upon activities through negotiation with the teacher; research, writing their own tricks, either found or invented, explaining and helping others, studying and adapting Worksheets and Texts and practising tricks (they may be advised to do this in secret at home). They may decide upon a suitable format for performance both within the class and for other people. They may subsequently discuss the varying success of different tricks or presentation.
All these choices may of course be adapted to suit other approaches. A similar variety also applies to the initial introduction of Magic given below.

Introducing Magic into the Classroom

1. Students work from 'cold' on the Introduction and Reading Passages (towards discussion and/or performance) – this may be useful if individuals finish their classwork early (higher levels).
2. The teacher performs tricks which require a large number of volunteers using the whole class, (e.g. Number Tricks – Section Two).
3. The teacher performs a trick which requires an assistant – and 'plants' a confederate amongst the spectators (see Confederate Tricks – Section Three).
4. The teacher performs his own favourite trick.

If the teacher employs a variety of approaches he will cater for the great diversity of learning styles (individuals and classes have their preferences but none are wholly consistent).

Notes are provided for each section to help the teacher organize the classroom, and enable him to fit tricks into his syllabus should a more formal approach orientated towards language goals (or stand-by) be chosen. Equipment needed for the tricks, implying associated vocabulary, and also language topics and organization are given.

The 'Speaking Skills' are adaptations of Wilkins' categories for a Notional Syllabus as may be found in many functional textbooks.

The 'Reading Skills' are lexical items necessary to perform the tricks (equivalents may be possible). These items are ones which I consider to be characteristic of tricks in a section and which are also more generally applicable to other situations. Some of the items may be considered common-core words (based on a frequency count) and others may go to make up a core vocabulary of words that collocate widely with many different words. This may be of benefit to students of ESP as well as those studying a more general course, as a vocabulary is provided with which the students may 'gloss' – make analogies or paraphrase more difficult matter in simple terms which they already know (see Hutchinson and Waters). I suggest the benefits of a core vocabulary outlined by Ron Carter may apply: 'It can be used for such everyday tasks as talking to children and foreigners, for summarizing, explaining things in a non-technical manner and communicating in a neutral and uncommitted way'.

Whilst not intending that all the Speaking and Reading Skills should be pre-taught the materials and activities may provide a useful context within which such items may be practised and/or used.

Choice of Tricks/Level

The *Contents* lists the tricks in each section. At the Recreation Stage students should be allowed to choose any tricks they wish so that they may be challenged, without being over-protected by the preconceptions of the teacher. Beginners may need help to simplify some of the tricks and more advanced students advised how to make them more complicated – both linguistically and practically. Performing the tricks is generally easier than reading, once they are understood, i.e. following a Practical Demonstration (Hutchinson). Should a more formal approach be chosen the suggested guidelines shown below may assist the choice of activities.

Level

Performance	–own trick or following practical demonstration (teacher or another student)	–Good Beginners and above
Reading for understanding	–following practical demonstration	–Beginners
	–without demonstration	–Intermediate
Writing/Tasks		–Beginners to Advanced.

However, the more communicative approach outlined above would concentrate on co-operation – group work and teacher assistance – to overcome such restrictions.

Things to Remember

1. Perform the trick once only on a particular day or ask someone else to perform one before you repeat yours. This will make it more interesting and less easy for the audience to guess the secret.
2. Take your time – generally the longer the trick, the more enjoyable it is.
3. Don't worry if things turn out slightly different when you are performing a trick. Take your time. It may still work.
4. Don't worry if things go completely wrong – failing can be *fun* too.
5. Remember the golden rule – let other magicians have a chance. You may think you know how a trick is done, but you may be wrong. Afterwards, you may advise the magician how he can improve his trick or help with linguistic difficulties.

Bibliography

Carter, Ron, 'A Note on Core Vocabulary'. First draft of a paper for the COBUILD project 1982 at the University of Birmingham.

Hutchinson, T., 'The Practical Demonstration', *Practical Papers in English Language Education*, Vol. 1, Institute for English Language Education, University of Lancaster, 1978.

Hutchinson, T., and Waters, A., 'Performance and Competence in English for Specific Purposes', *Applied Linguistics*, Spring 1981.

Johnson, K., and Morrow, K., *Communication in the Classroom*, Longman, 1981.

Wilkins, D.A., *Notional Syllabuses*, Oxford University Press, 1976.

PART THREE:

The Tricks

Section One: Dealing with Objects

Movement

UNIT A: Manipulation Tricks

Notes

Language Topics
Describing present states (position/colour), movement with parts of the body, talking about future actions.

Level

Performance	– Beginners
Reading	– following performance – Good Beginners
	– without performance – Good Intermediate
Writing/Tasks	– Intermediate/Advanced.

Summary
These tricks are quick starters to introduce magic if you or competent students perform them first. Minimal linguistic skill but some dexterity is required. Informal demonstration – 'off the cuff'.

Speaking Skills

Showing/introducing objects	– Look here's a . . .
	– This is a . . .
Calling for attention	– Watch carefully.
	– What colour is it?
	– Where is it?
Talking about future actions	– I'm going to . . .
Contradicting	– No it isn't. It's red.
	– No it isn't. It's here.
Asking someone to do something	– Pull it through your fingers.
Asking other people to try	– Would you like to try?
	– Have a go.

17

Reading Skills

Verbs	ask, blow, clench, contradict, cover, fold, give, give up, hold up, hurt, jump, lay, let, let go, make, make sure, point, practise, pretend, pull, put, rub, shake, spread, straighten, stretch, tell, tie, wait.
Prepositions	around, behind, between, from, over, to, together, towards.
Adverbs	automatically, carefully, quickly, secretly, sharply, thoroughly.
Equipment and Related Lexis	coloured rubber bands, several balls/pieces of coloured string, hands (fingers, thumb, wrist, knuckle), head, neck.

Introduction

A manipulation trick is a clever little trick that is performed skilfully with the hands – small objects can be made to jump or move in unusual ways.

In 'Manipulation Tricks' you do not have to say very much because your own hands do most of the work – just ask volunteers to try to do something or tell the spectators what you are going to do – and hey presto, perform the trick right in front of their eyes. Often you can repeat these tricks again and again as no-one guesses how to do them straight-away. Usually a small group is best unless everyone can see what you are doing.

For most of these tricks you do not need any help because you use your own hands, but 'What colour is this one?' shows you how other people from the audience can help you do a trick. Tricks, such as 'Here and There' need very little practice because they are almost automatic as long as you follow the instructions carefully.

You should be able to find all the equipment very easily.

Tasks for Students

Perhaps you can already do some clever things with your hands, but have you tried showing them to other people – using English? If you can do this, try teaching someone a manipulation trick – this is quite difficult if you do not touch the objects, but only explain what the other person must do. You can even write a Worksheet yourself.

If you do not know any tricks like these, ask your family and friends if they know any. They might be able to show you how to move objects around with your fingers. Then you will have to work out what to say (in English of course) before you show someone else your tricks.

Can you invent any new manipulation tricks?

Can you juggle?

WORKSHEET A: *'Here and There'*

Magic Trick:	Make a rubber band jump between your fingers.
Performance:	A quick trick with a small group – no help is needed.
Equipment:	A rubber band about $1\frac{1}{2}$ inches long.
Procedure:	Make a rubber band jump from your first two fingers to your third and fourth fingers by following these instructions:

(a) Hold up your hand with the back towards your audience.
(b) Put a rubber band over your first and second fingers as far as it will go (see Figure 1).
(c) Clench your fist and secretly stretch the rubber band over the tips of all your fingers (see Figure 2).
(d) Quickly straighten your fingers and, hey presto, the rubber band will automatically jump to your third and fourth fingers (see Figure 3).

Practise the trick until you can do it properly.

Presentation: *What to do*   *What to say*

Look, here's a rubber band. I'm going to put it over two fingers like this . . .

Figure 1   *Hold up the back of your hand and put the rubber band over the first two fingers.

I am now going to make it jump between my fingers.

Figure 2   Clench your fist and stretch it over all four fingers. Point to the rubber band.

Watch carefully! It's here now . . .

Figure 3   Straighten your fingers and the rubber band will jump.

Hey Presto! Now, it's there.

Figure 4   Now repeat the trick* and make the rubber band jump back to you.

Now I'm going to make it jump back again.

Give someone else the rubber band and let them try. Let other people try. Repeat the trick when you want to. Do not show/tell them the secret until you are ready.

Would you like to try? Come on. Have a go!

HERE AND THERE!

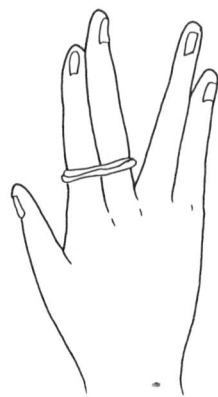

Figure 1

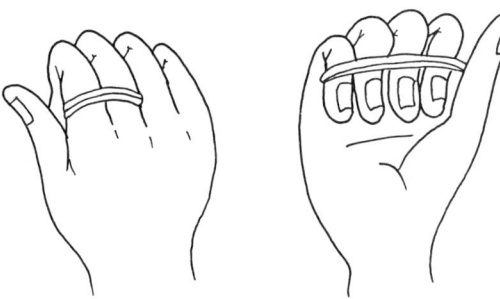

Figure 2

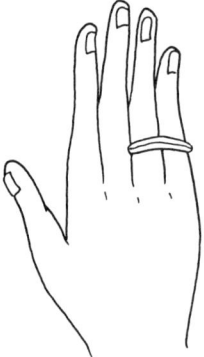

Figure 3

'All Change'

Magic Trick:	Now make two rubber bands jump between your fingers and change places.
Performance:	This is the follow-up to 'Here and There' – do it after Worksheet A. Again – a quick trick with a small group and no help is needed.

Equipment: Two or three differently coloured rubber bands about $1\frac{1}{2}$ inches long (*any colours).

Procedure: Tell your class you are going to make two rubber bands change places. Put a red* rubber band over your first two fingers and a blue* rubber band over your third and fourth fingers (Figure 1). Clench your fist (as in the Worksheet), and stretch both rubber bands over all your fingertips (see Figure 2). Tell your class to watch carefully and remember which side of your hand the red one and the blue one are. Straighten your fingers and, hey presto! the rubber bands change places. Continue repeating this trick as in the Worksheet.

Preparation: Before you do this trick, practise it carefully and work out what you are going to do and say, as in Worksheet A.

Note: Finally say that the trick is more difficult if you put a third rubber band (another colour – perhaps yellow) over all your fingers before clenching your fist in the usual way (Figure 3). Do this and the rubber bands still change places.

ALL CHANGE!

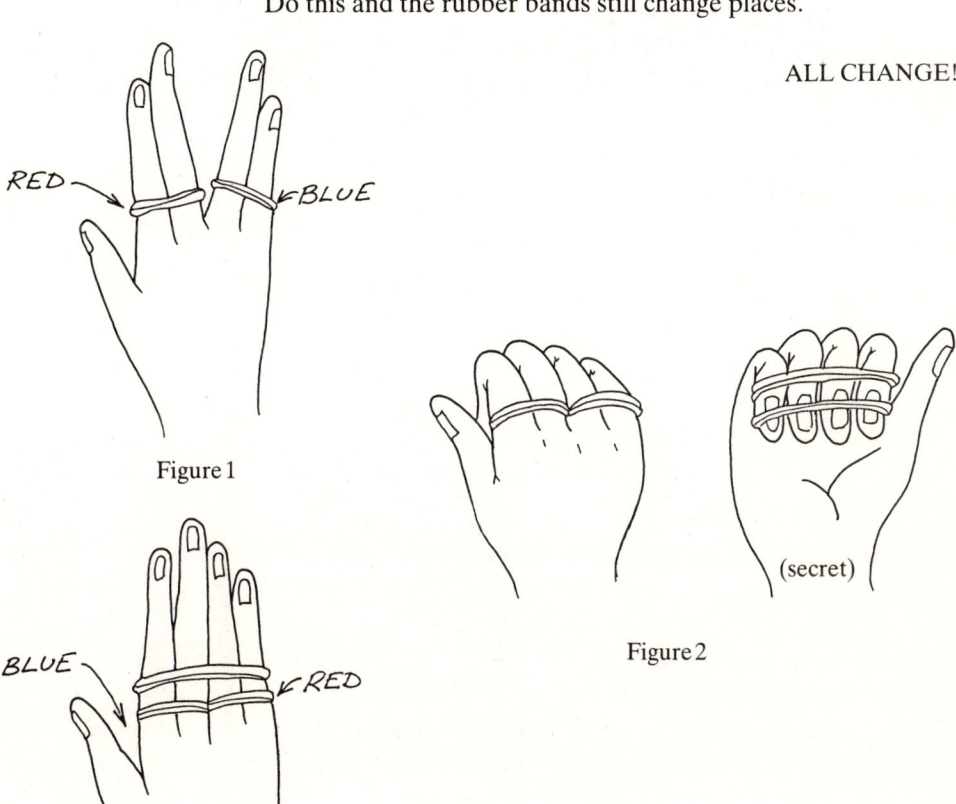

RED   BLUE

Figure 1

BLUE   RED

Figure 3

(secret)

Figure 2

'What Colour is This One?'

Magic Trick:	Make two different coloured pieces of string (round someone's wrist) change places.
Performance:	A quick trick with a small group and a helper.
Equipment:	Two different coloured pieces of string – each about 2 inches long, someone's wrist.
Procedure:	Tie the ends of one piece of string together to make a ring. Lay this ring over someone's wrist so that a loop hangs down each side. Now, pass the other string through each of these loops and tie the ends of this piece of string together. Hold the upper string with your right hand and the lower string with your left hand. Now ask, 'What colour is the string around his/her wrist?' Wait for the answer and then, as you say a magic word, let go with your left hand and pull sharply with your right hand – abracadabra – the strings change places. You can contradict your class and tell them what colour string is round his/her wrist now.
Preparation:	Practise the trick first. If you have several pieces of string you can put them round a ruler and ask about more than one at a time, e.g. 'What colour is this one?' or 'What colour is that one?'

WHAT COLOUR IS THIS ONE?

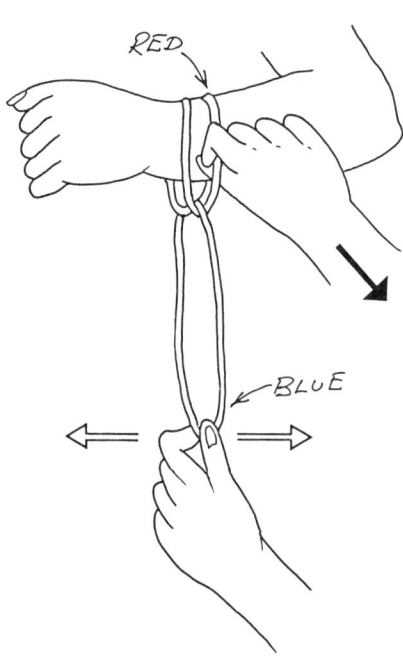

UNIT B: Join and Release

Notes

Language Topics
Asking about ability, explaining instructions.

Level
Performance   – Intermediate
Reading   – Intermediate
Writing/Tasks   – Beginners to Advanced.

Organization
Pair work or small informal groups. Some tricks larger groups with several volunteers.

Speaking Skills
Showing/introducing objects   – What are these?
Polite requests   – Would you . . .
Asking about ability   – Can anybody . . . ?
Reinforcing rules   – No, you must not . . .
Asking about physical states   – Are they linked now?

Reading Skills

Verbs	ask, clip, confuse, cut, escape, explain fail, fasten, fold, give, grip, hand, hold, join, jump, knot, link, move, pass, press, pull, put, release, remind, remove, slip, tear, try, tuck, (un)tie.
Prepositions	apart, away, between, from, in, of, off, on, over, round, through, to, together, under, up.
Adverbs	carefully, downwards, exactly, firmly, sharply, smoothly, upwards.
Adjectives	exposed, folded, left, right.
Equipment and Related Lexis	banknotes, handkerchieves, large paper-clips, a lot of pieces of string, rings or keys, large safety-pins.

Introduction

Magicians often push things together to make them link or join, and also pull things apart so that they separate from each other. Often large, shiny, metal rings, or other special equipment, are used. This section has similar tricks but instead of special equipment, ordinary objects such as safety-pins, paper-clips and handkerchieves are used as the 'props'.

Sometimes magicians knot rings onto strings in mysterious ways. This unit has one or two tricks like this, but they can be done with ordinary rings for fingers or even keys. The last trick in this unit uses string and people – the people are tied together with the string and have to escape from each other.

Tasks for Students

Try and find some more 'Join and Release Tricks'. For some of them you may have to make, or find, special props (such as large metal rings). Others need a lot of practice and skill before you can do them well, especially the string tricks.

1. Can you find out how to cut a piece of string in half and then join it together again?
2. Can you find out how to remove a number of keys knotted on a string when someone is holding both ends of the string?
3. Have you ever seen a picture of an escapologist? Sometimes they are tied up and locked in a strong box or even a bank safe. Ask a friend to tie your hands together and see how long it takes you to escape.
4. Can you find any tricks which help you to escape more quickly?
5. Can you find out how to escape from a waistcoat without removing your jacket?

Try and find some escapology tricks yourself, but don't practise them alone in case you really can't escape.

A very funny escapology trick for a magic show is to ask to be sellotaped up in a very large cardboard box (like the ones that refrigerators or washing-machines come in). Then try to escape from the box, but make it look very difficult and take a long time (five minutes at least) to escape. Groan a lot and roll the box about on the floor before escaping. Special clothes can help too – such as flying helmet and goggles!

WORKSHEET B: *'Jump to It!'*

Magic Trick:	Join or link two paper clips together without touching either of them.
Performance:	A longer trick with a small group – ask people if they can do it first.
Equipment:	Two large paper clips, a piece of paper folded in half (a bank-note borrowed from the audience is best).
Procedure:	Ask your students to try to link the two paper clips without holding them. You can do this trick by first clipping them onto a folded piece of paper (Figure 1). Then tuck the right hand end of the paper under the left hand paper clip (Figure 2). Sharply pull the two ends of the paper apart and the paper clips will jump together and you will see they are now linked. You can use some paper-money – perhaps your students will lend you a note.
Preparation:	Practise the trick in secret first.
Presentation:	*What to do*	*What to say*

What to do	*What to say*
Hold up the paper clips.	What are these? . . . Yes, that's right. They are paper clips. Would someone link/ join them together?
Hand the clips to a volunteer.	Here you are . . . Good. Now then, can you link them without holding them?

If he tries, remind him of the rules.
Ask the other people.

When everyone gives up, say:

. . . No! You must not hold them.
Can anybody link the paper clips without holding them?
I shall need some money. Can someone lend me some? . . . (No, not coins, a note please . . .) Thank you. If the trick works you can have your money back.
Watch carefully what I am doing.

Fold the note. Clip on the paper clips and tuck the right-hand end of the note under the left-hand paper clip.
Pull the ends of the note and make the clips jump together. Let other people try.

Now I am not holding the paper clips.
Would anyone else like to try?

Repeat: Do the trick again but explain exactly what to do.

Look, I shall show you again.

Note: If you tear the note, apologize.

Sorry. My magic was too strong.

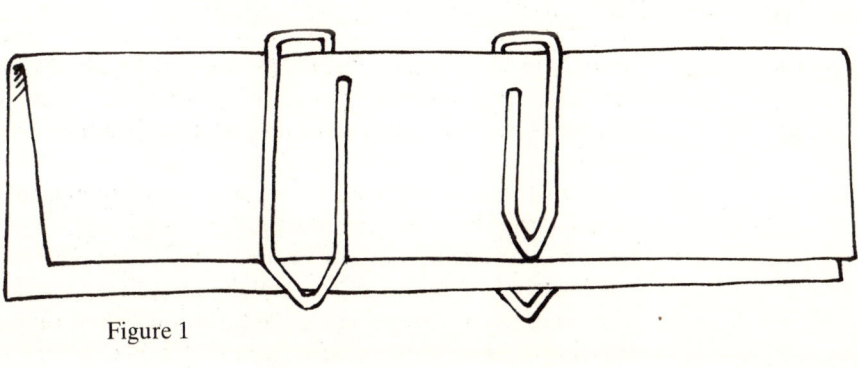

Figure 1

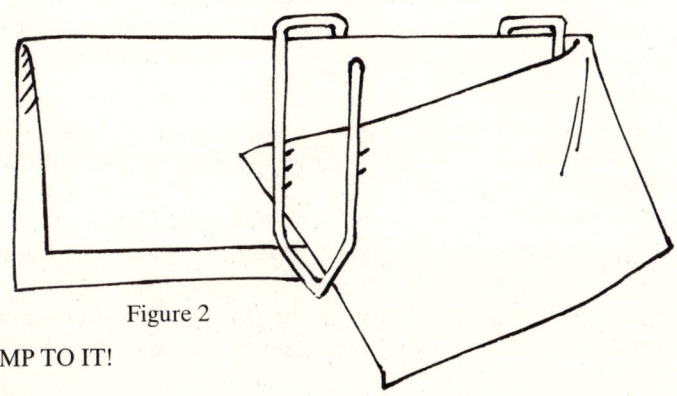

Figure 2

JUMP TO IT!

'Pull Them Apart'

Magic Trick:	Link two safety-pins together and then pull them apart without opening either of them.
Performance:	A quick trick with a small group.
Equipment:	Two large safety-pins (more if you want to teach others how to do the trick).

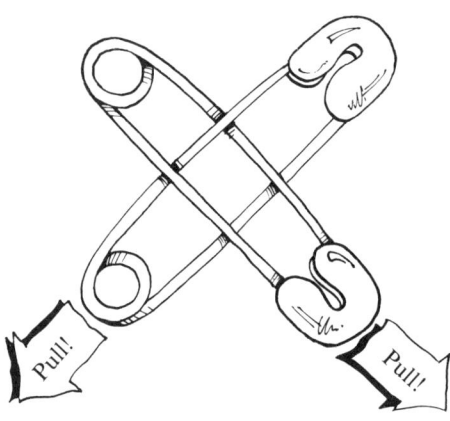

Procedure:	Get a student to link the two safety-pins together. Then, ask him/her to pull them apart without opening either of them. Ask other students to try. When everybody gives up, hold the safety-pins exactly as in the diagram and pull them apart sharply – hey presto, the pin moving to the right slips through the catch over the other pin, but neither opens completely. Let your class try again; they will probably fail as the pins must be held exactly as in the diagram. Show them the trick a few more times and, when you are ready, tell them exactly how to hold the safety-pins.
Preparation:	Be sure to practise this trick in advance and work out what to do and say.

'Don't Open It!'

Magic Trick:	Pin a safety-pin to a handkerchief and then take it out without opening the safety-pin.
Equipment:	A large safety-pin, a cotton handkerchief, a table.
Procedure:	Fold the handkerchief in half. Put the safety-pin once through both sides of the handkerchief at the fold (Figure 1). Ask your students to release the pin from the handkerchief without opening it. When they give up, demonstrate the following:

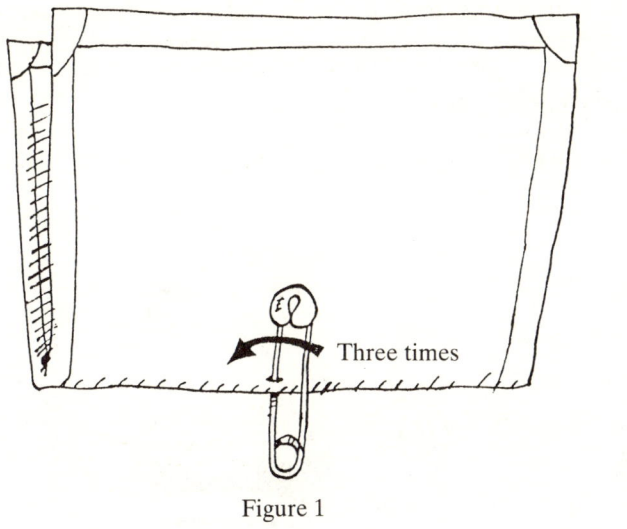

Three times

Figure 1

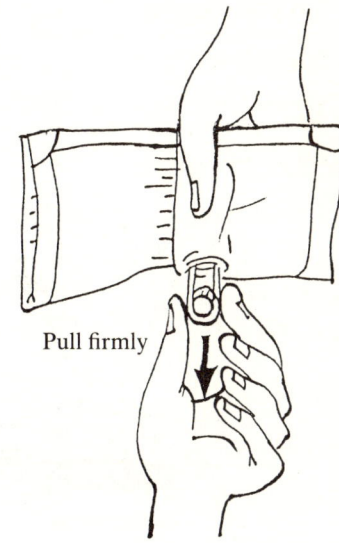

Pull firmly

Figure 2

Secret:	Turn the pin over carefully three times so that it is wrapped up in the handkerchief. Press down on the handkerchief just beyond the covered end of the pin. Grip the exposed end of the pin firmly and pull it smoothly away from the handkerchief (Figure 2) – Hey presto, the pin just slides out but it's still closed.
Repeat:	Again, let your students try. Show them again and if they still can't do it, explain exactly what to do.
Preparation:	Don't forget to practise the trick before your presentation and work out what to do and say.

'Knot the Ring!'

Magic Trick:	Put a ring on a piece of string and tie a knot on the ring, without letting go of the ends of the string.
Performance:	A longer trick with a large audience and some volunteers.
Equipment:	Several rings-for-fingers (or keys if you like) and some pieces of string about one metre long (a ring and a string for each volunteer).
Procedure:	Give each person a piece of string and tell them to put their ring (or key) on it – that's easy. Now tell them hold both ends of their string and knot the ring onto the string, but without letting go of the ends – that doesn't sound so easy. Let them try for a few minutes and when you are ready show them how it's done like this:
	Put a ring on your string and put it on the table in front of you. Fold your arms and then hold both ends of your string.

Now, without letting go of the ends, unfold your arms carefully and move your hands apart – the ring is now knotted onto the string.

Preparation: Try it for yourself first.

KNOT THE RING!

'Magic Handcuffs'

Magic Trick:	You and your partner are handcuffed together, but you can escape from him without untying the handcuffs.
Performance:	A long trick, a large group, several volunteers in pairs and a volunteer who will be handcuffed to you.
Equipment:	Some pieces of string one metre long – each pair of volunteers will need two pieces. You will need two pieces of string, too.
Procedure:	Ask for a volunteer and tie the ends of a piece of string around each of his wrists to make handcuffs. Repeat this with another volunteer, but before tying his second wrist, pass the string over and under his partner's handcuffs to interlink them

(Figure 1). Repeat this for other pairs of volunteers. Now, ask the pairs if they can escape from each other, but without un-tying the knots, cutting the strings or taking them off their wrists. Let everyone try to escape for as long as they like; while this is going on handcuff another volunteer to yourself in the same way. In the end everyone will probably give up. Then follow these instructions to release yourself from your partner: Point your hands upwards and ask your assistant to point his hands downwards (Figure 2).

Take the middle of his string and pass it up through your right handcuff (Figure 3).

Keep pulling this string through until there is a loop big enough to put your fingers through. Pass this loop over your right hand. Let go of the string and pull your hands apart – you are now separated (Figure 4).

Preparation: Be sure to practise this first and work out exactly what instructions to give when you are helping other people to escape.

THE MAGIC HANDCUFFS

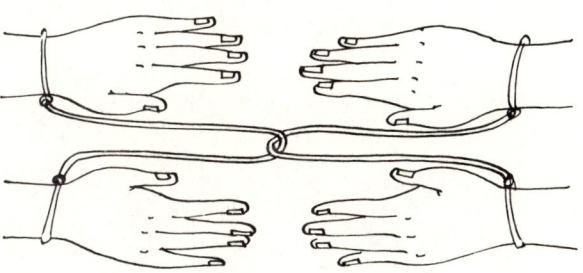

Figure 1

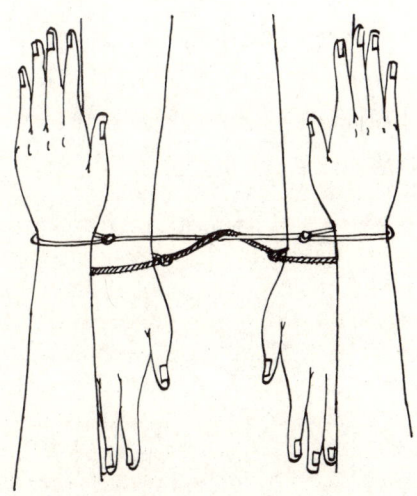

Figure 2

THE MAGIC HANDCUFFS

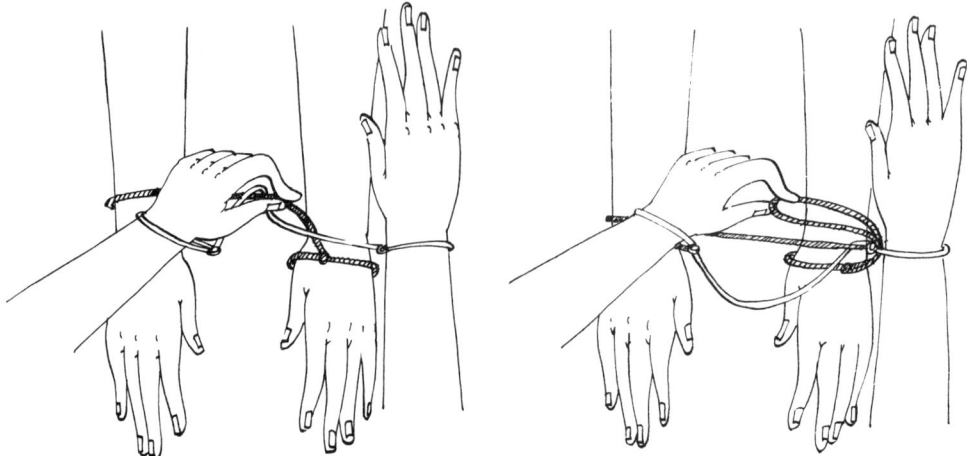

Figure 3

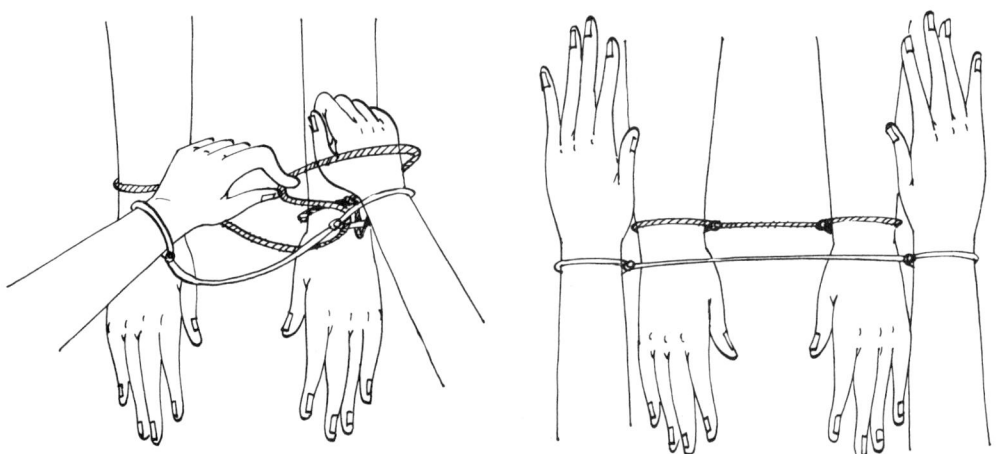

Figure 4

Properties and Positions

UNIT C: Impossible Tricks

Notes

Language Topics
Giving instructions; describing actions; talking about success and failure.

Level

Performance	– Good Beginners and above
Reading	– Intermediate
Writing/Tasks	– Beginners to Advanced.

Organization
Small informal groups, several volunteers.

Speaking Skills

Giving instructions	– Please fill this glass.
Asking about ability	– See if you can . . .
Talking about failure	– I'm afraid it's sunk.
Reinforcing rules	– It must float . . .
Describing actions	– I put it on the water.
Polite request	– Would anyone else like to . . .
Distributing objects	– Here is a straw.
	– Here are some more pins.

Reading Skills

Verbs	blend, blow, deflate, encourage, fill, find, float, give, leave, lie, lift, make, need, push, put, (re)light, rub, show, slide, sink, stand, tell, tie, touch, untie, use, work.
Prepositions	in, inside, into, near, on, out, over, to, up.
Adverbs	careful, hard, quickly, steadily.
Adjectives	coated, covered, exhausted, horizontal, round.
Equipment and Related Lexis	balloon, (three) bottle(s), candle, cup, large dictionary, glasses, jug of water, matches, paper bag, straw, tissue paper.

Introduction

Your spectators will probably find these tricks impossible, but you can do them because of the properties of the chosen objects, i.e. they sink, float or allow you to lift other objects. The last two tricks in this unit ('Blow it Out' and 'Blow it Over') involve the properties of air.

Try asking your students to do these impossible tricks first. They will probably fail to do them so you can show them how they are done. Occasionally (as in 'Sink or Swim' part two) you can show a trick but keep the secret to yourself.

Tasks for Students

When magicians do 'Impossible' tricks they often make them more exciting by making them dangerous (such as fire eating) or expensive (such as plate spinning). Do not attempt such tricks unless you and your teacher are well insured. Instead try to find some 'Impossible' tricks that you can perform in the classroom.

For instance:

1. Can you make a boiled egg float and then sink again? (A Chemistry trick)
2. Can you stick a pin in a balloon without bursting it? (A Physics trick)
3. Can you make water change into wine? (A Chemistry trick)
4. Can you force a hard-boiled egg into a carafe (a wide-necked bottle)? (A Physics trick)
5. Can you turn a glass of water upside down without spilling it? (A Physics trick)
6. Can you make invisible ink? (A Chemistry trick)
7. Can you write a worksheet/text for an 'impossible' trick?

If you study science or have access to a library and can find some Chemistry or Physics books, you may be able to invent some new 'Impossible' tricks. But make sure they are not too expensive or dangerous.

WORKSHEET C: *'Sink or Swim?'*

Magic Trick:	Two ways to make a pin float on water.
Performance:	A long trick with a small group, and some volunteers.
Equipment:	A jug of water, two drinking glasses, a few small squares of tissue paper, a candle (which you use before you do the trick) and a few pins.
Procedure:	This is really two tricks – one which you explain to your class and one which you don't explain.
	1. If you put a pin on the surface of the water it will sink to the bottom. If you first put a pin on a piece of tissue paper and *carefully* put the tissue paper on the surface of the water, the tissue paper will sink but the pin will float on the surface.
	2. If you give another pin a wax coating by rubbing it well on the candle, that will also float – but don't tell your class.
Preparation:	Practise in secret and be sure you can do both tricks. When you are ready, put the jug of water, one glass and most of the pins in the middle of the table. Put the tissue paper and the wax covered pin in the other glass at the side.
Presentation:	*What to do* *What to say*

Say to one of your class: What's this? . . . Yes, that's right. It's a jug – a jug of water.

Ask someone else:

> Please fill this glass for me . . . Thank you.

Give a pin to someone.

> This is an ordinary pin. See if you can float it on top of the water.

Let someone else try.

> I'm afraid it's sunk to the bottom. Would you like to try. Here's another pin . . . It must float on the surface of the water.

When you are ready, put a pin on some tissue paper. Carefully put it on the water.

> Look, I'll show you how to do it. Here's a pin . . . I put it on the water carefully. Look the tissue paper sinks, but the pin floats.

Let other people try.
Give out the pins and the tissue paper but leave the waxed pin in the glass.

> Would anyone else like to try? Here are some more pins and some tissue paper . . .

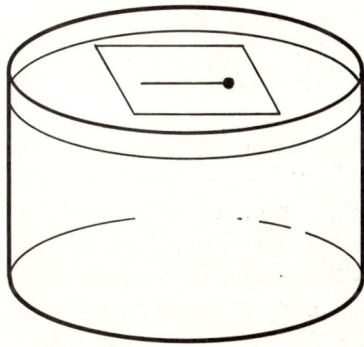

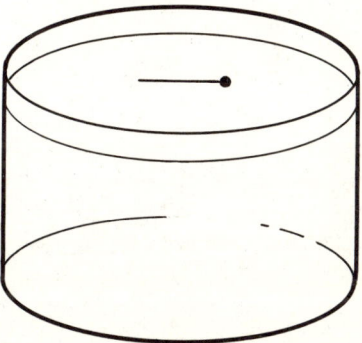

When you are ready, do the trick with the wax-coated pin.

Quickly pour all the water (and the pin) back into the jug and go on to another trick.

Here is another pin . . . This time I'll use a magic word instead of tissue paper . . .   Abracadabra! Look my pin is floating – that's magic for you!
Now, I'll say the magic word again and it will sink. Abracadabra!

'Lift It Up!'

Magic Trick:	Lift a glass bottle with a drinking straw.
Performance:	A longer trick with a large group and some volunteers.
Equipment:	A glass bottle, a ruler and several drinking straws (use one at a time).

LIFT IT UP!

Procedure: Ask your students if they can lift up the bottle using only a drinking straw. Let them try and when they give up show them how, like this:

Bend the drinking straw so that one end is slightly longer than the diameter of the bottle. Then push this end into the neck of the bottle. Lift the other end of the straw and the bent end will be pressed against the sides of the bottle in a horizontal position. This allows you to lift the bottle using only the straw.

Preparation: After some practice you should not need the ruler.

'Blow It Up!'

Magic Trick: Lift an inflated balloon with a cup. Then lift the cup with the balloon.

Procedure: A longer trick with a large group and some volunteers.

Equipment: A cup and a balloon.

Procedure 1:   Blow up the balloon and tie the neck with some string (so that you can untie it). Then, ask your class to lift up the balloon with the cup, without touching the balloon with their hands. Let them try and then show them how it's done. Blow gently on the balloon and hold the cup against the other side of it. Then blow onto the top of the balloon and slide the cup underneath it. Continue blowing and you will find that you can lift the balloon with the cup.

Procedure 2:   Ask your students if they can lift the cup with the balloon and nothing else. When they give up, show them how to do it. Untie the string, deflate the balloon. Place it inside the cup and then blow it up again. The cup should then stick to the inflated balloon so that you can lift it with the balloon and nothing else.

Preparation: Try it for yourself in secret.

'Blow It Out!'

Magic Trick:	Blow out a candle which is behind a glass bottle.
Performance:	Quite a quick trick with a large group and some volunteers.
Equipment:	A candle in a holder, some matches and a large round bottle (or three bottles).

Procedure:	Ask a student to put the candle in the holder and light the candle. Now, ask someone else to blow it out – that's easy. Then re-light the candle and place one of the large bottles in front of it. Now ask someone to blow out the candle without removing the bottle – that doesn't sound so easy. In fact, it is simple – if you blow steadily and hard against the bottle air currents are sent round the bottle and abracadabra, the candle just goes out.
Preparation:	Try it and see. If you are clever and practise you may be able to use two or three bottles in a row in front of the candle – it will still go out.

'Blow It Over!'

Magic Trick:	Blow over a big fat book which is standing on one end.
Performance:	A quick trick with a large group and several volunteers.
Equipment:	A big, heavy book such as a dictionary or encyclopaedia, a table and a paper bag.
Procedure:	Stand the book on the table and ask someone if they can blow it over. Ask someone else to try and then encourage other people to join in so that several people are blowing at the same time. When everyone is exhausted take the paper bag out of your pocket and lie it flat on the table, near the edge. Stand the book on it. Now, blow into the bag – and abracadabra! – over it goes.

Preparation: Try it for yourself first and find the right book. Then, work out what to do and say.

UNIT D: Construction Tricks

Notes

Language Topics
Asking about ability; describing actions; talking about success; guessing.

Level
Performance   – Beginners and above
Reading   – Intermediate
Writing/Tasks   – Beginners to Advanced.

Organization
Small informal groups or large informal group for practical demonstration. Quite long tricks.

Speaking Skills

Checking vocabulary	– What are these?
Asking about ability	– Can anyone make . . . ?
Asking for a volunteer	– Would someone like to try?
Giving instructions	– First make the bridge . . .
Talking about success/failure	– I'm sorry . . .
Describing actions	– Now fold it lengthwise like this.
Guessing	– How many are there now?

Reading Skills

Verbs	ask, cut, draw, finish, follow, get, give, hold, interlock, join, let, make, move, open, point, put, (re)arrange, remove, place, seem, show, sit, stand, strengthen, support, take, try, turn, twist.
Adverbs	carefully, downwards, upside-down, upwards
Prepositions	across, along, between, next, on, out.
Adjectives	big, bottom, empty, equal, fresh, full, half, little, long, new, numbers, small, top.
Equipment and Related Lexis	Ten coins, four glasses, knives, large newspapers, A4 paper, scissors, water.

Introduction

These are all engineering tricks. They are similar to *Impossible Tricks* but are concerned with position of objects as well as their properties. The first two tricks ('Magic Paper' and 'A Sharp Trick!') both involve making bridges. The third trick ('Point It Up!') involves re-arranging coins to make a new pattern. The fourth trick ('How Many Are There?') involves asking people questions about what you have made.

Tasks for Students

Can you find any *Construction Tricks* where magicians make things? How about these?

1. Tricks which use matches or coins (or coasters with a large group) to make shapes
    – Can you place five coins on the table so that each one touches the other four?
    – Can you arrange six matches to make four triangles?
2. Can you balance a needle on the head of a pin? (You will need some extra equipment for this one.)
3. Can you make a fir tree or a ladder out of a newspaper?
4. Can you make a hole in a postcard, big enough to walk through?
5. Can you make anything using origami – the ancient Japanese art of paper folding?
6. Try asking your friends about optical illusions – pictures that puzzle your eyes.
7. Can you invent any *Construction Tricks* of your own – engineering or craft books may help. Then try writing a worksheet or text to tell someone how to make something in a magical way.

WORKSHEET D: *'Magic Paper'*

Magic Trick:	Make a bridge out of a piece of paper, strong enough to stand a glass on.
Performance:	A longer trick with a large group and some volunteers.
Equipment:	Three drinking glasses and several sheets of A4 writing paper.
Procedure:	Put the three glasses in a row, almost touching each other and then carefully remove the middle one. Now ask your students to make a paper bridge between the two remaining glasses strong enough to stand the third one on (Figure 1). The paper seems much too weak to hold the weight of a glass, but you can strengthen it by folding the paper over and over to make many little pleats (Figure 2), and, hey presto! the paper bridge is now strong enough to support the glass.
Preparation:	Practise it first and make sure that the unfolded paper is not strong enough, but that the pleated paper is.
Presentation:	

What to do	*What to say*
Put the glasses in a row, almost touching each other.	What are these? . . . Yes, that's right./No, they are glasses.
Remove the middle one.	Now, can anyone make a bridge out of this piece of paper and stand his glass on it?
Give him the piece of paper and the glass.	*Would someone like to try? . . .
	Here you are. First make the bridge. Right, now stand the glass on it.

*Ask someone else

> I'm sorry. I'm afraid it hasn't worked.
> Would someone else like to try?

When you are ready, take the piece of paper and show them how to do it.

> Right, Give me the paper. Now, fold it lengthwise like this to make lots of little pleats.

Give someone a fresh piece of paper and let them try.

> I put the bridge over the two glasses. Now, very carefully you can stand the glass on it like this . . . Hey presto! Right. Now can you do it? Would you like to try?

MAGIC PAPER

Figure 1

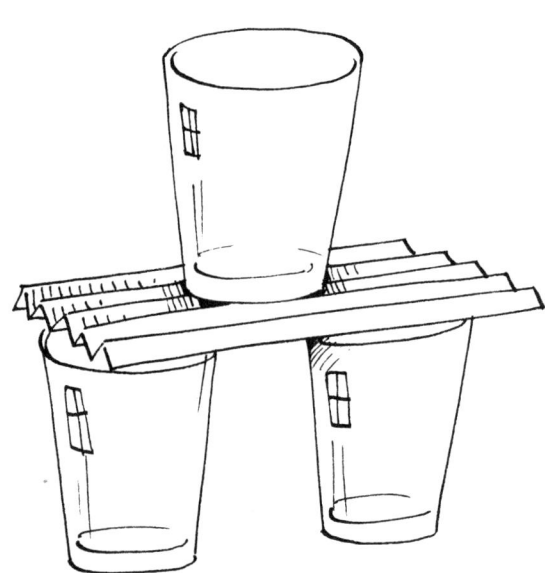

Figure 2

'A Sharp Trick!'

Magic Trick:	Make a bridge out of three knives, strong enough to stand a glass of water on.
Performance:	A longer trick with a large group and some volunteers.
Equipment:	Three knives, three empty glasses and a glass of water.
Procedure:	Turn the empty glasses upside-down and stand them on a table so that they make a triangle with equal sides. The sides of the triangle should be slightly longer than the knives (Figure 1). Now, ask your students to make a bridge out of the knives and stand the full glass of water on it. There are two rules:

1. The empty glasses must not be moved;
2. No part of any knife may touch the table.

Let your students try first. Then, when you are ready, inter-lock the blades of the knives and place a knife-handle on each of the three empty glasses (Figure 2 – from above). Hey presto! You can now sit the full glass of water on the bridge.

Preparation:	Make sure you can do the trick and know what to say first.

A SHARP TRICK

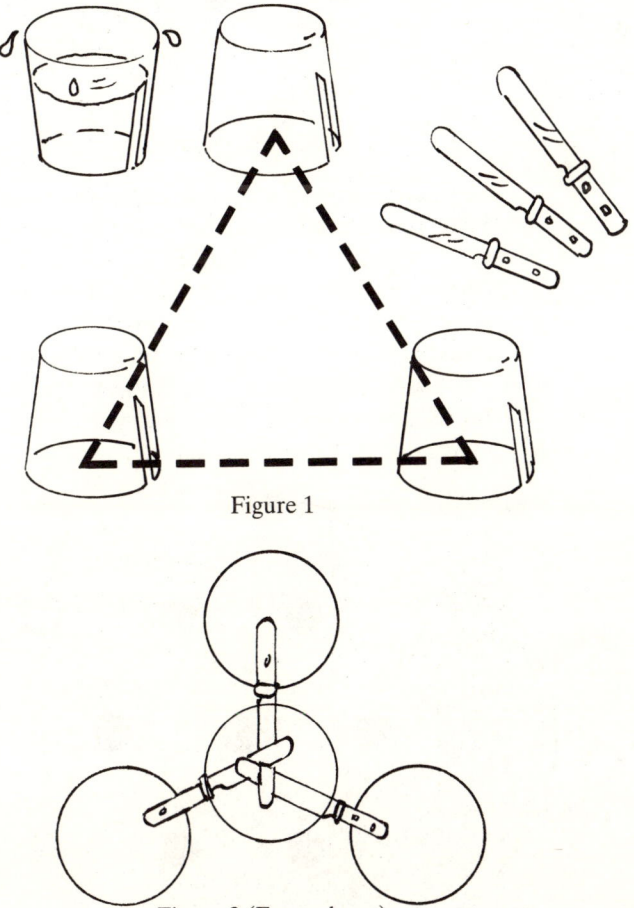

Figure 1

Figure 2 (From above)

'Point It Up!'

Magic Trick:	Re-arrange a triangle of coins so that it is pointing up instead of down.
Performance:	A quick trick with a small group.
Equipment:	Ten coins of the same value.
Preparation:	Arrange the ten coins in a triangle which is pointing downwards for the spectators, i.e. four coins in the top row, three coins in the next, two in the next, and one at the bottom.

POINT IT UP!

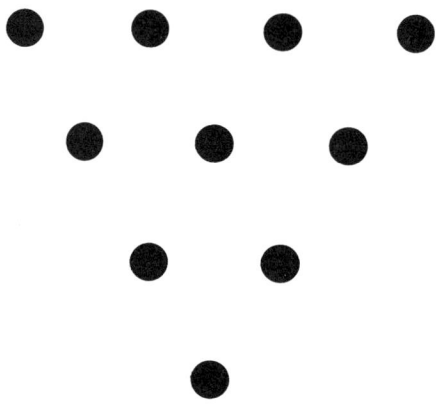

Figure 1

Procedure:	Ask your class if they can make the triangle point upwards instead of down, by only moving three coins. Let them try and then show them the solution.
Solution:	Move the coin at the bottom round the triangle until it is just above the middle of the top row – this will be the new point of the triangle. Move the two coins on the longest row down two rows to make the new bottom row. The triangle now points upwards instead of down but you have only moved three coins.

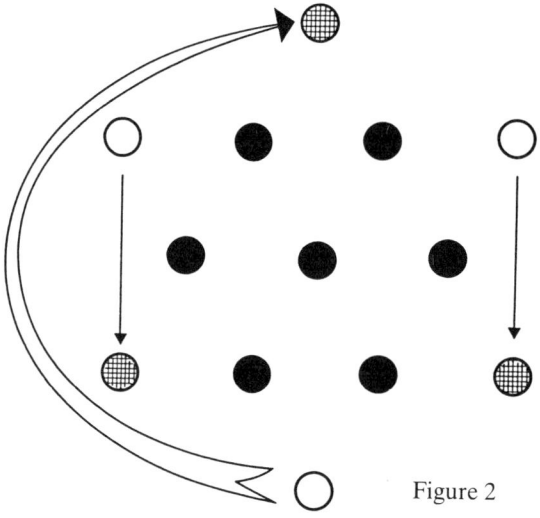

Figure 2

'How Many Are There?'

Magic Trick:	Cut rings of newspaper down the middle to end up with a different number of rings.
Performance:	A long trick with any size group.
Equipment:	Four double sheets from a large newspaper and a pair of scissors, some sellotape.
Preparation:	Cut the sheets diagonally to make strips about 2½ inches wide.
Procedure:	

1. Take the first strip and draw a line along the middle on both sides. Next join the two ends to make a ring – without twisting it. Cut along the line. When you have finished hold the paper in one hand and ask the spectators 'How many rings are there?' and 'What are they like?' Then open out the paper to show two rings of equal size. Of course the spectators guessed right.

2. Take the second strip and draw a line along the middle on both sides. Next give one end a half twist before joining it to the other end to make a ring. Cut along the line. When you have finished ask the same questions. Some people will probably be wrong – there is just one very large ring.

3. Take the third strip and repeat the procedure but this time give one end a full twist before joining it. Cut along the line and ask the questions. This time there are two rings of the same size but they are joined together.

4. Draw a line one third of the way across (instead of along the middle) the fourth strip on both sides. Give the paper a half twist and cut along the line – this will take you twice as long as before – just keep following the line. While you are cutting ask 'What will I get this time?' You get one very big loop joined to a small ring.

HOW MANY ARE THERE?

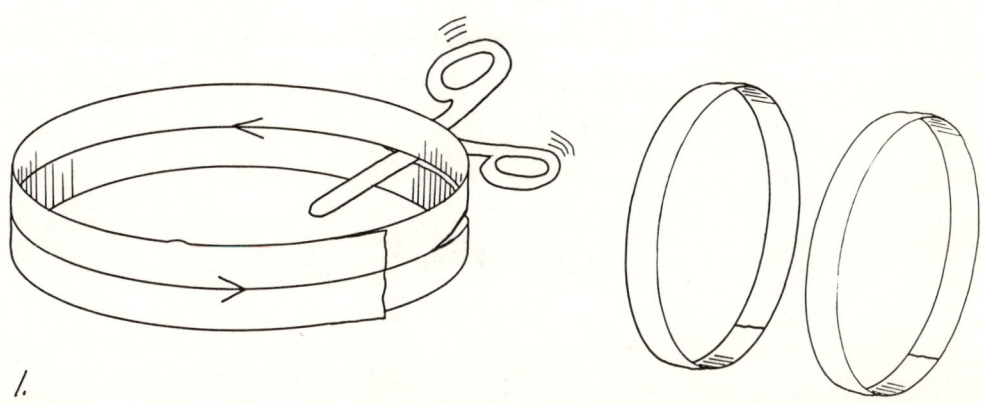

1.

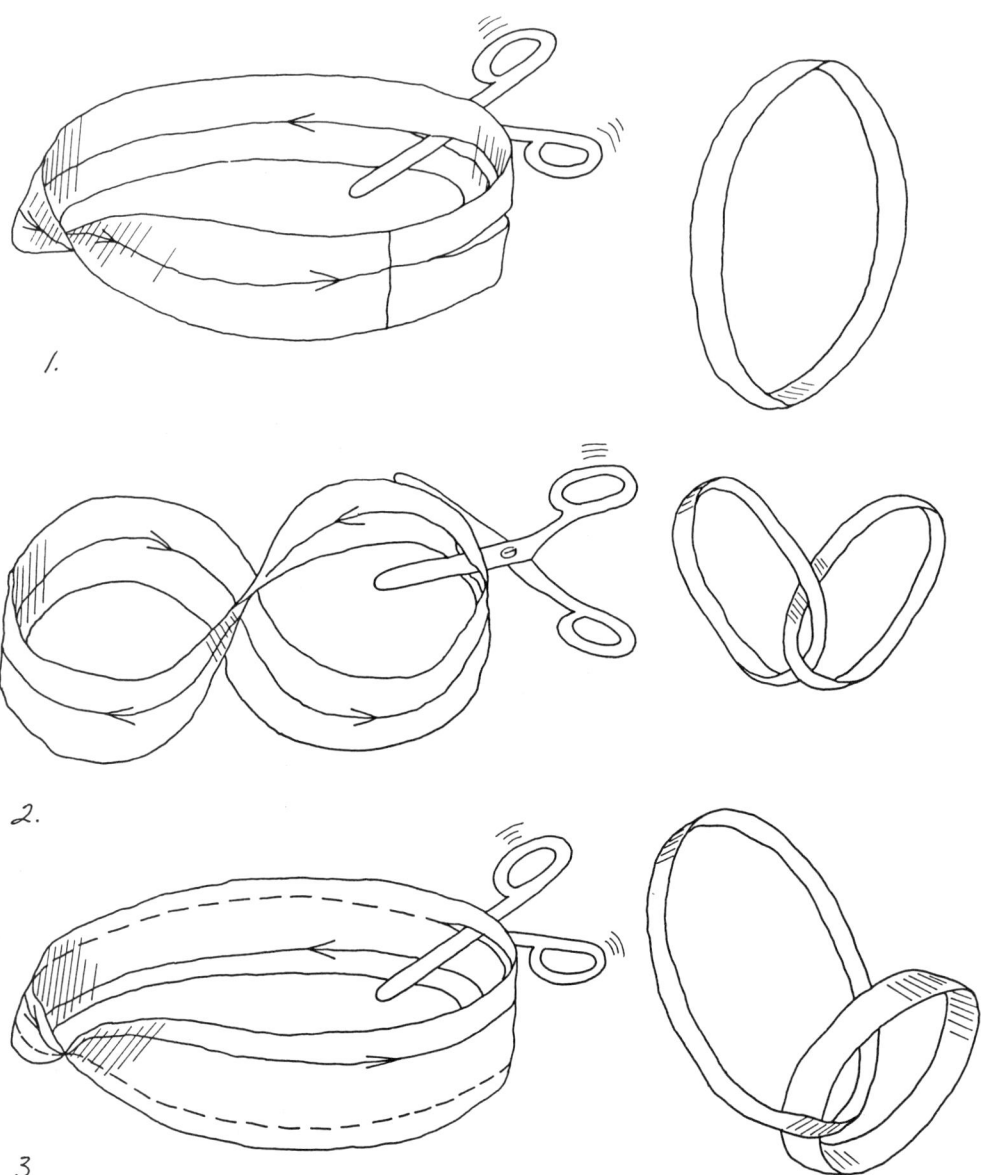

1.

2.

3.

UNIT E: Location Tricks

Notes

Language Topics
Talking about performance; giving instructions; identifying objects.

Level
Performance   – Good Beginners/Intermediate
Reading   – Good Intermediate
Writing/Tasks   – Beginners to Advanced.

Organization
Larger informal groups, slightly harder tricks because more organization and reading.

Speaking Skills
Alternative ways of asking   – And this?/How about this?
Giving instructions   – Please check . . .
Guessing   – Hmm, I think this is the square.
Reading aloud   – This one says . . .
Identifying objects   – This is the one.

Reading Skills

Verbs	arrange, ask, divide, draw, examine, feel, fit, fold, give, glance, grasp, handle, hold, indicate, inspect, join, lend, let, mix, move, pass, pretend, put, read, remember, remove, repeat, return, search, shake, show, (sub)divide, surprise, take, tear, think, touch, try, (un)clasp, write.
Prepositions	by, from, in, into, on, onto, out, under, up, with.
Adverbs	carefully, exactly, hard, lightly, quickly, slightly.
Adjectives	chosen, cool, firm, hard, middle, numbers, position (e.g. top right hand corner), rough, soft, warm, well-known.
Equipment and Related Lexis	paper bag, nine different books, box, coins, envelopes (cards to fit them), firm oranges, felt-tip pen, pencil, pack of playing cards, ruler, saucers, scissors, watch or ring.

Introduction

These are tricks where you decide upon the location of an object which has been chosen by the spectators. Pretend to use your magical powers or E.S.P. (extra-sensory perception) to determine which object was chosen by your spectators when you were not present.

For the first four tricks ('Which is Which?', 'Hard Oranges', 'The Warmest One' and 'Rough Edges') the way something feels tells you the location of the chosen object. In the next two tricks ('Which One?' and 'Where Oh Where?') your assistant tells you the position of the chosen object by using secret hand signals which you have agreed beforehand. The last two tricks ('Take a Card' and 'The Eleventh Card') are simple card tricks where you can tell which card was chosen. There are many more difficult card tricks than these.

Once you are sure that you know the location of the chosen object then you can make the trick seem much more difficult by calling for silence so that you can concentrate and use your magical powers. It also looks harder if you take a long time before you tell the spectators what you have decided. If you want, you can ask them to think hard about the chosen objects to help you too (mindreading).

Tasks for Students

Try to find some more tricks which use location:
1. Card tricks which use thick, bent or narrow cards.
2. Attach a hair from your head onto a coin and see if you can work out a trick.
3. If you can feel that similar looking objects are different or you can think of ways to get your assistant to signal which objects have been chosen you should be able to invent some location tricks of your own.

Try writing a worksheet or text to tell someone how to perform a *Location Trick*.

WORKSHEET E: *'Which is Which?'*

Magic Trick:	When you are blindfolded you can tell what is drawn on a card which is inside an envelope.
Performance:	A long trick with a large group.
Equipment:	Four rectangular envelopes and cards which fit them exactly (the bigger the group the larger the envelopes), a scarf for a blindfold. Some extra cards for doing it again.
Preparation:	Draw a circle on the first card, draw a square on the second one, on the third one a triangle and on the fourth one a rectangle.

When the cards have been put in the envelopes and mixed up you can surprise your class by telling them which card is in which envelope. The secret is that you can *feel* which is in which envelope, because the card with the circle on it fits exactly but you have trimmed the other cards like this:

card with square – 1mm from a vertical side (it will move from side to side slightly) card with triangle – 1mm from the top side (it will move up and down slightly)

card with rectangle – 1mm from a vertical side *and* 1mm from the top (side to side and up and down).

Prepare the extra cards in the same way, put them in order and keep them in fours.

Presentation:	*What to do*	*What to say*
	Give out the cards to different people.	What's this? . . . Yes/No – it's a square. And this? . . . Yes/No – it's a circle.
		How about this? . . . Yes/No – a triangle. This one? . . . Yes/No – it's a rectangle.
	Give each person an envelope to inspect.	Here are some envelopes. Please check that they are just ordinary envelopes and when you are satisfied put in your card and tuck in the flap.
	Ask people to mix them up on the table.	Please put the envelopes on the table. Now will you mix them up until you are sure I don't know which is which. Anyone else? . . .
	Ask other people to inspect them.	And you? . . . And you? . . .
		Now, pass them around and check the envelopes are identical and have not been marked in any way.
	Give someone the scarf and ask to be blindfolded.	Now will someone blindfold me so that I definitely cannot see . . . Are you sure I can't see? . . .
	Ask for an envelope, feel it and pretend to think hard. Give it to someone to check.	Give me any envelope . . . Hmm. I think this is the . . . Here . . . open it. Am I right?
	Repeat with the second one. And the third one.	. . . good.
	Now the fourth one.	Give me another one please . . . This one is either the . . . or the . . . Ah, it's the . . . This one must be the . . .

Repeat:	Repeat the trick or ask people to draw well-known objects on a new set of four cards, e.g. a car, a house, a man and a tree.

'Hard Oranges!'

Magic Trick:	Pick the marked orange out of a bag containing several others.
Performance:	Quite a long trick with a large or small group.
Equipment:	A large bag, some small firm oranges (or tangerines) on a dish and a felt-tip pen.
Procedure:	Pass the dish of oranges to a student and ask him to mark one orange with the felt-tip pen and then pass the dish back to you. Ask someone else to hold the bag open for you. Now tell your class that you are going to inspect all the oranges very carefully so that you can remember which one is the marked one. Pick up the oranges one by one, turn each one over in your hands, look at it carefully and put it in the bag. Now ask your student to shake the bag to mix up the oranges and hold it up so that you can't see inside. Ask everyone to think about the marked orange – and, hey presto, take it out of the bag. Remove this orange and let someone else try.
Secret:	The secret is that when you examine the oranges you handle them all very carefully except for the marked one. You give this orange a hard squeeze so that when it is in the bag, you can feel it is much softer than the others.
Preparation:	Practise this trick at home with your own oranges. Make sure the ones you show your class are firm to begin with. Think of a good reason for removing the marked orange (e.g. it's tired now) before letting your class try the trick.

'The Warmest One'

Magic Trick:	Pick out the marked coin from a bag containing several others.
Performance:	A quick trick with a fairly large group.
Equipment:	Several coins of the same size and value, a small bag, a saucer and a felt-tip pen.
Procedure:	Give someone the bag to hold. Then, pass the saucer round and ask your class to lend you some coins of the same value (e.g. 1p pieces). Next ask someone to choose a coin from the saucer and tip the others into the bag. The chosen coin is then marked with the felt-tip and passed round for everyone to examine before it is put in the bag with the others. The bag is shaken and then, although you can't see inside, you quickly put your hand in – and, hey presto, pull out the marked coin. Pass the coin round again for people to examine, put all the coins back on the saucer and repeat the trick after a few minutes.

Secret:	The secret is that your students handle the coin when they examine it. This means that when it is in the bag, you can feel it is much warmer than all the other coins – but you must be quick!
Preparation:	Practise it with a student and feel the coins quickly before the marked one has time to get cool.

'Rough Edges'

Magic Trick:	Pick someone's word out of a box which contains nine slips of paper which all have different words on.
Performance:	A longer trick with a large group and ten volunteers.
Equipment:	Some sheets of paper with smooth edges, a pencil, ruler and a box.

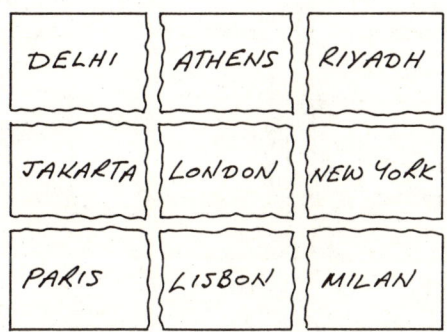

Procedure:	Take a piece of paper, divide each side into three with the ruler and join the opposite marks to make nine squares. Fold along the horizontal lines and tear the paper into three strips. Then fold along the vertical lines and tear so that you have nine small squares. Give these out to nine students and ask them to write a word or name on their piece of paper, fold it in half and put it in the box. Now ask someone else to shake the box and hold it up so that you can't see in. Put your hand in the box and feel around. Tell someone to think hard about the word or name which he wrote to help you find his piece of paper – Abracadabra! You pull out a slip and read the word on it and it's the right one.
Secret:	The secret is that the student you chose is the one who wrote on the middle square which is the only one with four rough edges. When you put your hand in the box you could identify this one by feeling the edges.
Repeat:	Repeat this trick with nine more small pieces of paper, but give someone else the middle one.
Preparation:	Be sure to practise it first.

'Which One?'

Magic Trick:	Identify which book was chosen from a total of nine books.
Performance:	A longer trick with any size group and *an assistant*.
Equipment:	Nine different books carefully arranged on the table.

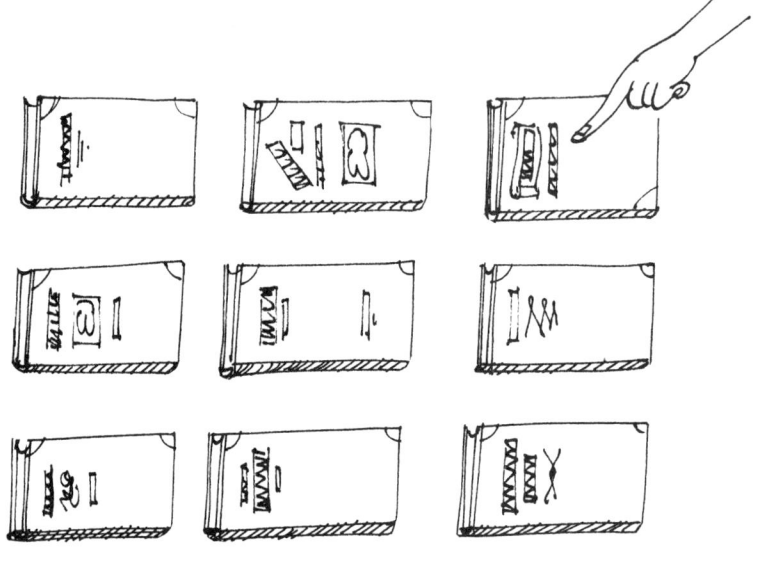

Figure 1

Procedure:	Ask your assistant to arrange the nine books in three rows of three (Figure 1). Tell your audience that you want them to choose one of the books when you are out of the room. When you return your assistant touches the books in any order and asks you if that book was chosen.
	Your assistant tells you which book was chosen by the position of his/her finger on the first book he/she touches – if he/she touches the middle of the first book then the middle book was chosen – if he/she touches the top right-hand corner of the first book then your class chose the book in the top right-hand corner and so on.
Preparation:	Practise with your assistant. When you repeat the trick don't wait until he/she touches the right book but, after he/she has touched one or two, interrupt him and say 'I think you chose that one' and point to the right one yourself.

'Where? Oh, Where?'

Magic Trick:	You and your assistant can find any object which is hidden in the room much faster than anybody else.
Performance:	A long trick with a large group and *an assistant*.
Equipment:	Any small object e.g. a watch or a ring.

	1	2
1 finger	**2**	
	3	4
3 fingers	4 fingers	

Procedure:	You and your assistant decide what you are going to hide somewhere in the room. Then your assistant goes out while someone hides it. When he/she returns, you indicate, secretly (only to him/her), which quarter of the room the hidden object is in by grasping an agreed number of fingers in your right hand. When he/she goes to that area you indicate which quarter of that area the object is in by unclasping your hands and then grasping the new number of fingers. Continue sub-dividing the new areas until your assistant has only a very small area to search. He may then have to look under other objects, but should be much quicker than anyone else who tries apart from yourself.
Preparation:	Practise this trick with your assistant and take turns to go out of the room. Let other people try and time everyone with a watch to see who is quickest – your assistant and yourself should always win.

'Take a Card'

Magic Trick:	Find the card which a student chose.
Performance:	A quick trick with a small group.
Equipment:	A pack of playing cards.
Presentation:	Shuffle the pack of cards and hold them out to someone to choose a card. Tell him/her to take one and remember it. Cut the pack (into two halves) and ask him/her to replace his/her card in the pack without telling you which card he/she chose. Shuffle the cards (mix them up) and then deal them out into one pile on the table. When you reach his/her card tell him/her.
Secret:	The secret is that when you cut the pack you glance at the bottom card of the top pack. You then shuffle the cards lightly, taking care not to separate these two cards. When you deal the cards onto the table you know that the card he/she chose must be the next one after the one you have remembered.
Repeat:	Try and see if anyone else knows any different card tricks before you repeat this.

'The Eleventh Card'

Magic Trick:	Identify which card has been chosen from a full pack of playing cards.
Performance:	A long trick with a small group and a volunteer.
Equipment:	A full pack of fifty-two playing cards, excluding the jokers.
Procedure:	Deal out twenty-one cards, face up, into three small packs of seven cards each. As you are doing this, ask the volunteer to remember one card and then tell you which of the three packs it is in. Put this pack between the other two, turn the cards over and deal out the same twenty-one cards into three small packs of seven cards each. Again ask the volunteer to identify the pack containing his/her card and put this pack between the other two. Repeat this process twice more, so that you have dealt out the cards four times altogether.
	When the volunteer has told you which pack contains his/her card for the fourth time, again put this pack between the other two and then, this time, turn up the cards one by one. Pretend to think carefully about each card you turn up – the volunteer's card will be the eleventh one.
Note:	On no account should you shuffle the cards during this trick.
Preparation:	Practise this with an assistant first.

Vanishing

UNIT F: Vanishing Tricks

Notes

Language Topics
Giving instructions; apologizing; asking about position.

Level

Performance	– Beginners and above
Reading	– Intermediate
Writing/Tasks	– Beginners to Advanced.

Organization
Pair and informal group work. 'Rub It Away' more difficult text.

Speaking Skills

Naming objects	– What's this? . . .
Giving instructions	– Now roll it up.
Helping	– Say the magic word.
Apologizing	– Sorry, it hasn't disappeared.
Asking about position	– Where has it gone?
Astonishment	– Amazing!
Making excuses	– Perhaps it's the wrong . . .

Reading Skills

Verbs	apologize, ask, borrow, bunch, can, check, contain, convince, fly, fold, follow, hide, hold, lean, mark, pick, point, pretend, pull, put, rely, repeat, roll, rotate, rub, say, scratch, slip, spread, stretch, take, transfer, try.
Prepositions	away, behind, down, in, inside, on, out, towards, up, with.
Adverbs	convincingly, horizontally, slightly.
Adjectives	left, right, top.
Equipment and Related Lexis	coins, drinking glass, handkerchieves, jacket, paper napkin, felt-tip pen, pencils, table.

Introduction

Magicians are well-known for the magical way they make things disappear, become invisible or vanish. There are hundreds of tricks like these which use many different objects. Here are a few tricks which show some of the ways *Vanishing Tricks* can be performed in the classroom.

The first trick in this section ('The Disappearing Pencil') depends on the position of objects. The other three tricks ('The Vanishing Pencil', 'The Jumping Coin' and 'Rub It Away') are all manipulation tricks.

Every time you make a different object vanish the spectators think you are performing a different trick as you never let them in on the secret. Generally speaking the quicker the trick, the more chance there is of the audience spotting how it is done because they are all concentrating hard. Also, the longer the trick, the more interesting and the more fun it is to do and watch.

Tasks for Students

1. Make a list of all the *Vanishing Tricks* you can think of or find and the objects that you use.
2. Try to make these tricks as long as possible by the things you say and do. Remember if you have an identical object hidden away you can make things reappear too – anywhere you like.
3. Try putting a duplicate coin in a sealed envelope inside a book.
4. If you are clever you can also 'plant' objects in people's pockets as they come into the room.
5. You can also tell the audience that an object has become invisible and pretend to watch it fly round the room before you eventually go and find it.
6. Try using different objects for similar tricks and then try to write a worksheet or text.

WORKSHEET F: *'The Disappearing Pencil'*

Magic Trick:	Make a pencil disappear (or vanish) by rolling it up in a handkerchief.
Performance:	A longer trick with a small audience and a volunteer.
Equipment:	A pencil and a cotton handkerchief.

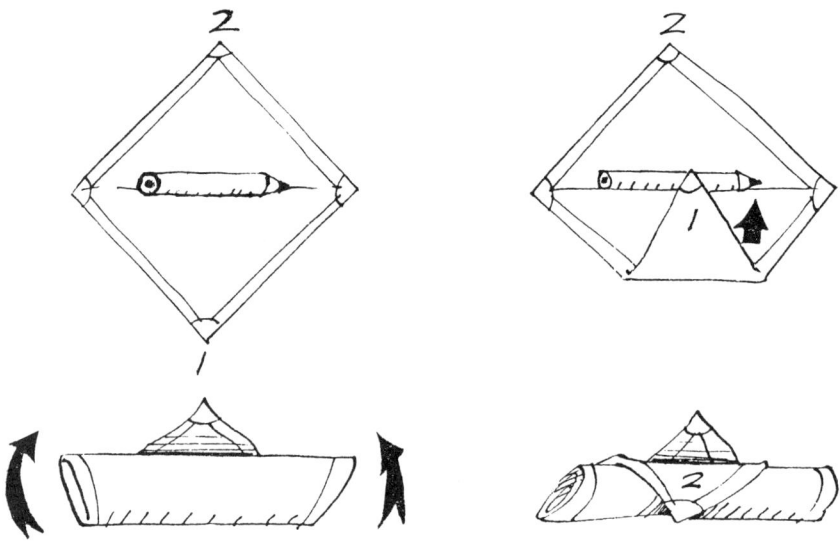

Procedure:

You can make a pencil 'disappear' by rolling it up in a handkerchief. In fact, you have only made the pencil go under the handkerchief. Look at the diagrams and practise it first.

Presentation:

What to do | *What to say*

Put the handkerchief down on the table, and hold up the pencil.

> What's this? . . . Yes/No – it's a handkerchief.
> And this? . . . Yes/No – it's a pencil.

Ask someone to put the pencil on the handkerchief and roll it up.

> Please put this on the handkerchief and roll it up . . .
> Thank you.

Say to the same person:

> Now, can you make it disappear? Say the magic word – Abracadabra. Now the pencil has disappeared. Please open the handkerchief and see . . .

Ask someone else to try.

> Oh, sorry it hasn't disappeared. It's still there. Would you like to try? Here you are. Roll up the pencil . . . Say Abracadabra. Has it disappeared? . . . No, sorry, it hasn't worked.

Then you try.

> Abracadabra . . . No, something is wrong. It still isn't working.
> Perhaps it's the wrong magic word. I'll try something else.

Try again. This time follow these instructions: Fold corner 1 over the pencil so that it slightly overlaps corner 2. Roll up the pencil. Stop when you can see corner 2 again.
Hold corner 1 with one hand and pull corner 2 back towards you with the other.
Ask someone.

> Hey presto. Look the pencil has disappeared.

> Have you got it? . . . No? Well where has it gone? . . . Amazing! It's gone right through the handkerchief.

Pick up the handkerchief and shake it.

Repeat:

Repeat the magic trick using the wrong magic word again; let someone else try, or go on to another trick.

'The Vanishing Pencil'

Magic Trick:	Make a pencil vanish by covering it with a handkerchief.
Performance:	A very quick trick with a fairly large group.
Equipment:	A pencil, a large handkerchief and a jacket with a wide sleeve.
Procedure:	Put the pencil under the handkerchief and hold it up so that its shape can be seen. Your students are surprised when you take the handkerchief away with your other hand as the pencil has vanished. In fact, you have been pointing your forefinger up, just like a pencil, under the handkerchief and the pencil has slipped down your sleeve.
Preparation:	Practise this in front of a mirror until you can do it convincingly. If you hide an identical pencil somewhere else, you can also make the pencil reappear – work out what to do and say as before.

'The Jumping Coin'

Magic Trick:	Make a coin jump from your handkerchief to your pocket.
Performance:	A quick trick, with a large or small group.
Equipment:	Two identical coins with the same date, a square handkerchief and your pocket.
Procedure:	Show someone one of the coins and ask him to remember the date. Then, spread the handkerchief on the table and put the coin in the middle. Fold the bottom corner to the top corner to make a triangle (Figure 1). Then fold the left corner A up past the top corner (Figure 2) and the right corner B, up past the top corner (Figure 3). Next hold corner B in your right hand and corner A in your left hand. Smoothly pull your hands apart and upwards until the handkerchief is stretched horizontally in front of you (Figure 4). Abracadabra! – the coin has disappeared.
	The secret is that the coin is still there, but it is hidden in the folds of the handkerchief. Bunch up the handkerchief carefully and put it in your pocket. Now put your hand in your other pocket, take out the coin and ask if it's the same date.
Preparation:	This trick is similar to 'The Disappearing Pencil' (see Worksheet F), but you must practise it carefully to do it well. If you want you can pretend that the coin has flown behind the cupboard or under the clock – where you have hidden the other coin of course.

'THE JUMPING COIN'

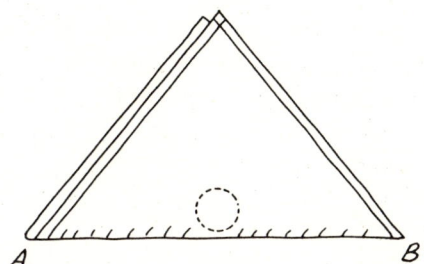

Figure 1

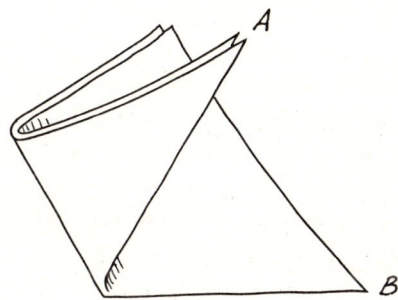

Figure 2

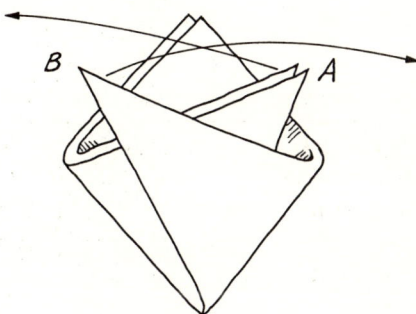

Figure 3

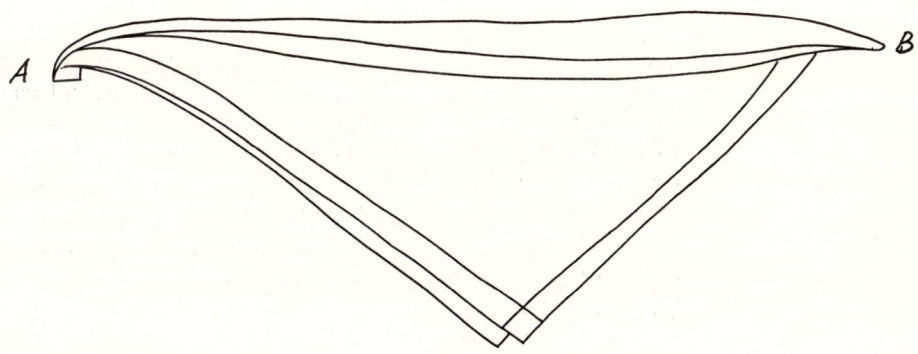

Figure 4

'Rub It Away'

Magic Trick:	Make a coin disappear by rubbing it on your fore-arm.
Performance:	A longer trick with a small group.
Equipment:	A shirt (or blouse) with a collar which you are wearing, a coin borrowed from someone and a felt-tip pen.
Procedure:	Borrow a coin from someone and ask them to mark it with the felt-tip pen. Then roll up your sleeves and tell the audience that you are going to rub the coin on your arm and make it disappear. Pick up the coin with your right hand and transfer it to your left hand. Then put your right hand round the back of your neck and lean on the table with your right elbow. Next rub the coin, which is in your left palm, up and down on your right forearm to 'try to make it disappear'. Pull your left hand away smartly and – 'Sorry, something went wrong' – the coin just clatters on the table. Apologize to your spectators and assure them that the trick will work properly next time. Keep on repeating this, making sure that every time you pick up the coin with your right hand, you transfer it to your left hand and rub your left hand on your right forearm. When you are sure that everyone is convinced that you can't do the trick, do it right; pick up the coin with your right hand and this time *pretend* to transfer it to your left hand. When you put your right hand round the back of your neck put the coin inside your collar. Go on to rub your left hand (which everyone thinks contains the coin) on your forearm and, abracadabra, when you pull your left hand away the coin has disappeared. Stretch both arms out in front of you and rotate your hands to show that the coin really has gone.
	Some time later, scratch the back of your neck with your *left* hand and pick up the coin. You can tell the spectators it was behind your ear or put it somewhere else first. Finally, let someone check that it's the same coin.
Preparation:	This trick relies on routine – make sure you practise it first. Try to convince your spectators that you really don't understand why it didn't work and think of different ways to apologise and make excuses.

UNIT G: Hidden Objects

Notes

Language Topics
Talking about appearance; giving instructions; contradicting.

Level

Performance	– Beginners and above
Reading	– Intermediate
Writing/Tasks	– Beginners to Advanced.

Organization
Some preparation and assistants, larger groups or practical demonstration. 'Unwind the Wool' is a more difficult text.

Speaking Skills

Naming objects	– What's this?
Talking about appearance	– Is it broken?
Giving instructions	– Now break it.
Checking	– Are you sure it's broken?
Contradicting	– No, you're wrong . . .

Reading Skills

Verbs	appear, ask, borrow, break, check, cover, drop, feel, forget, gather, give, glue, hide, hold, inspect, leave, lend, lift, look, make, mark, mend, open, place, protrude, pull, put, roll, return, say, show, slide, slip, tell, think, throw, turn, (un)fold, (un)wind, wave.
Prepositions	at, between, from, in, inside, on, over, round, up.
Adverbs	easily, slowly, tightly.
Adjectives	another, fake, flat, real, round, stiff, upright.
Equipment and Related Lexis	bin, cupboard, coin, glue, handkerchieves, matches, newspaper, (red) paint, paper, pencils, ball of wool.

Introduction

Here are some ways of making things disappear and then reappear, reappear mended after they have been broken or simply changed. These tricks all need careful preparation.

A. For tricks like 'Mend the Match' first hide ordinary objects in ordinary places – in this case a match hidden in the hem of a handkerchief. This is the way that magicians destroy someone's watch with a hammer and then make it reappear unbroken – I don't advise you to try this!

B. For tricks like 'The Empty Paper' first make special equipment with a secret pocket to hide things in. If you show the equipment empty first you can make things appear 'out of thin air'. Magicians use special equipment with secret pockets a lot. They have even used tricks like this to make an elephant disappear!

C. For tricks like 'Tear It Up' you must first make fake objects, objects which look real but which can be easily destroyed or changed.

D. 'Unwind the Wool' uses a special slide (a cardboard tube) to make things reappear in unexpected places.

Tasks for Students

Try and find out how to do these tricks or work them out:

A. 1. Can you hide an apple under an orange skin?
    2. Can you make a coin appear out of an ordinary matchbox?
    3. Can you cut a piece of string in half and then join it together again?
B. 4. Can you use 'the empty pocket' to double someone's money or use it to change a coin into a bank-note?
    5. Can you make some special equipment with a secret pocket to make a handkerchief appear out of an empty paper-bag? (Use two paper-bags, one inside the other, and some glue.) Try making a magic tube too.
    6. Can you make a secret pocket in a bag made out of material? (Black velvet works best as you can't see the stitches.)
    7. Find out how to make boxes or hats which have false bottoms to hide things in.
C. 8. Can you find out how to make a machine for changing pieces of paper into bank-notes?
    9. Can you make a fake 'red' pencil which changes colour when you wipe it with a handkerchief?
   10. Can you make any other fake objects which you can destroy or 'vanish' (try using things that come in packets – remember the audience must believe that the objects are real first by the way they sound, feel, look or work).
D. 11. Can you use the cardboard slide to make things reappear inside small boxes held together with rubber bands? (Pull out the slide and the boxes will snap shut.)
   12. Can you use the cardboard slide to make a coin reappear inside a loaf of bread?

Other tricks also use very fine thread which the spectators can't see to make things disappear and reappear or make things rise off the table in a mysterious way.

WORKSHEET G: *'Mend the Match!'*

Magic Trick:	Mend a match which is hidden in the folds of a handkerchief.
Performance:	Quite a quick trick with a small group and two or three volunteers.
Equipment:	Two matches and a handkerchief with a wide hem.
Preparation:	Hide one match inside the hem of the handkerchief.
Procedure:	Hold up the handkerchief but cover the match hidden in the hem with one hand. Ask someone to inspect a match and place it on the handkerchief. Fold the handkerchief over the match

and turn everything over, but hold the match hidden in the hem. Ask someone to break the match – Abracadabra! Open the handkerchief and you've mended it again.

Presentation:	*What to do*	*What to say*
	Hold up the handkerchief, but don't show the hidden match.	What's this? . . .
	Hold up the other match.	Yes, that's right./No, that's wrong. It's a handkerchief. And what's this? . . .
	Give this match to someone to look at.	Yes, that's right./No, that's wrong. It's a match. Look at it! – Is it broken? . . .
	Say to someone else:	No, it isn't. Good!
	Fold the handkerchief over the match, turn everything upside down, but hold the match hidden in the hem. Ask someone to break it. *(He/she breaks the hidden match but thinks it is the other one.)	Please put the match on the handkerchief. Now, break the match please. Is it broken? Good.
	Ask someone else:	Are you sure it's broken? Feel it . . . Good. No, you're wrong. It isn't broken. Look, I've mended it!
	Put the handkerchief down and slowly open it to show the unbroken match.	
Repeat:	Do the trick again with another match in the hem of a handkerchief or ask someone else to try (without a match in the hem).	

'The Empty Paper!'

Magic Trick:	Make a coin disappear and return again in five minutes' time.
Performance:	A long trick with a fairly large group.
Equipment:	Two squares of paper stuck back-to-back, a large book and somebody's coin.
Procedure:	Ask someone to lend you a coin. Take a folded piece of paper from your pocket and open it out on the table. Then, place the coin on the paper and fold it up again. Wave the paper in the air and open it up again – Abracadabra! The coin has gone. Fold up the paper again and put it under a book. Tell the audience that the coin has disappeared, but that it will come back again in five minutes' time if no-one looks under the book. Leave the book and get on with something else. When five minutes are up, tell everyone to come and look. Lift the

book and unfold the paper – Hey presto, the coin has returned.

Preparation: The secret of this trick lies in the preparation:

Take both of the pieces of paper and fold them into nine squares. Then, glue the centre squares together. Fold each sheet back-to-back so that you make two pockets – one at the front and one at the back. Of course, the coin doesn't really disappear, you just turn the paper over and open the empty pocket. To make the coin reappear, just turn the paper over again.

"THE EMPTY PAPER"

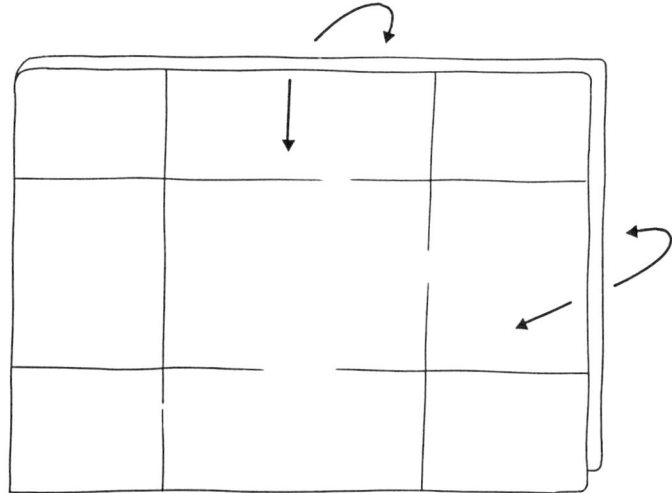

'Tear It Up!'

Magic Trick:	Tear up a pencil which is rolled up in a newspaper – then make it reappear.
Performance:	A quick trick with a large or small group.
Equipment:	A bin, a newspaper, two very short pencils (one sharpened at one end), some paper, glue and red paint. Another normal-size red pencil.
Procedure:	Pick up a pencil, wave it in the air, tap the point on the table and then roll it up tightly in a sheet of newspaper. Tell the audience that you are going to make the pencil vanish. Hold up the rolled up newspaper and tear it up inch by inch – Hey presto, the pencil has disappeared. Now take another sheet of newspaper and open it up – Hey presto, the pencil has reappeared inside this new sheet. Quickly gather up all the newspaper and throw it in the bin. Go on to something else.
Preparation:	The secret lies in the preparation. You make the fake pencil out of the two short pieces, the paper and the glue. Paint this pencil red. Then hide another real red pencil in the other sheet of newspaper. You can, of course, make it reappear anywhere you like by hiding it where you choose. Round pencils are best – have them both the same colour, so that people can't tell the difference between them.

'Unwind the Wool'

Magic Trick:	Make a coin vanish after you have folded it in a piece of paper. A few minutes later find the same coin in a ball of wool.
Performance:	A longer trick with a large group who are facing you.
Equipment:	A coin borrowed from the audience, a felt-tip pen, a piece of stiff paper 10cm x 15cm and your pocket which contains a ball of wool (or string) wrapped round a cardboard tube.
Preparation:	Make a flat cardboard tube, large enough to drop the coin in. Then wrap the ball of wool round the tube so that one end just protrudes. Check that the wool is not wound too tightly and that you can easily remove the tube with one hand. Put this 'magic' ball of wool in your pocket.
Procedure:	Borrow a coin from the audience and ask someone to mark it with the felt-tip pen. Put the coin in the middle of the paper and fold the sides over it – not too tightly (Figure 1). Ask someone to feel it and check it is still there. Put the paper in your left hand with your fingers facing the audience and fold the top down with your right hand as the coin slips into your left palm (Figure 2). Then fold the bottom up and grasp the packet in your right hand so that you can show your friends. At the same time, drop your left arm to your left side and drop the coin into your left pocket. Pass the folded piece of paper to

someone. He will be very surprised that the coin is no longer inside (Figure 3).

Forget about the coin and let someone else perform another trick or do one yourself. Then, put your left hand in your pocket, slide the coin into the tube and, keeping it upright, pull the tube out of the ball of wool. A few minutes later take the wool out of your pocket and ask someone to unwind it for you. Of course, the missing coin is inside.

UNWIND THE WOOL

Figure 1

Figure 2

Figure 3

UNIT H: Deception

Notes

Language Topics
Guessing about states; contradicting.

Level

Performance	– Intermediate and above
Reading	–Intermediate
Writing/Tasks	– Beginners to Advanced.

Organization
More difficult tricks as they are more open-ended, or complex. Practical demonstration or informal group work.

Speaking Skills

Naming objects	– What's this? . . .
Asking people to guess	– Which one do you think has matches in?
Asking people to do things	– Listen to this.
Talking about states	– It's full/It's empty.
Contradicting	– You're all wrong . . .

Reading Skills

Verbs	apologize, bend, bring, conceal, confuse, cut, empty, exchange, finish, gather, give, guess, join, leave, let, look, lower, notice, pick, practise, prepare, pretend, put, raise, rattle, repeat, shake, sit, slide, slip, show, smash, sound, spread, take, tear, think, try, turn, twist, work, wrap.
Prepositions	in, into, on, onto, out, over, through, up.
Equipment and Related Lexis	drinking glass, paper handkerchieves, matchboxes, napkin, rubber-bands, scissors, sellotape, table.

Introduction

These tricks are designed to confuse your audience. They all use hidden objects but also need quick thinking and some acting ability too.

'The Magic Matchboxes' uses a box hidden up your sleeve which rattles. It also makes use of the fact that an empty box and a box which is completely full never rattle. Your audience have to guess which box contains matches. You must decide what to say quickly as sometimes they will guess correctly and sometimes they will be wrong. 'Which Way Up?' is a similar trick but you must prepare the matchboxes first to make it more difficult for the audience to guess correctly. You need some acting ability for 'Right Through the Table' as you must make a paper napkin look as though it has a glass under it and convince your audience that it is really there. In 'Found Out' you make the audience believe they know how the trick works and then confuse them again as you have hidden an extra object.

Tasks for Students

Try and find some longer vanishing tricks or ones where you can confuse your audience.

1. Can you find a similar trick to 'The Magic Matchboxes' which uses coloured cards?
2. Can you find any story-telling tricks? There are some which use cards. Do you know the card trick where the jacks go to rob a country house? Ask your teacher if he knows this one.
3. Can you think of stories for any other tricks?
4. You can also confuse your audience if you use objects (such as cards) which have patterns on. Put a very small mark on the back of a card and you can watch where it goes but your audience don't know what to look for.

WORKSHEET H: *'The Magic Matchboxes'*

Magic Trick:	Confuse your class by shaking three matchboxes – sometimes they appear to have matches in, but sometimes they seem to be empty.
Performance:	A long trick with a large group and several volunteers.
Equipment:	Three boxes of matches on the table – one empty, one half-full and one completely full (so that it will not rattle) and another box of matches which is half-full and kept up your right sleeve by a rubber-band round your arm.
Procedure:	When you pick up the half-full box of matches it always rattles. When you pick up one of the other matchboxes they never rattle (as one is empty and one is completely full) except when you shake them with your right hand.
Preparation:	Practise this trick yourself first and work out exactly what you want to do and say.

Presentation:

What to do	*What to say*
Carefully put the boxes on the table in a line.	What are these? . . . Yes/No, they are matchboxes.
Ask two people to guess which box has matches in it.	Right, would you point to the box which has matches in it. This one? Right. And which one do you think has matches in it . . . ? That one? Good.
Now pick up the other box and shake it hard with your right hand – it will always rattle because you have got the box up your sleeve.	Sorry, I'm afraid you're wrong. Listen, this one has matches in . . .
Slide the boxes about on the table and repeat the trick – sometimes use your right hand so that they are always	Sorry, you're wrong again/ Perhaps you're right this time. . . . Yes, you are/No, you aren't.

wrong, sometimes use your left hand so they are sometimes right.

To finish the trick rattle each box in turn (with your right hand) and ask several people to guess how many matches there are in each box.

Good. Now listen to this box . . . How many matches do you think there are in this box?

Would you open the box and count the matches please . . . It's full./It's empty./There are . . . matches. You're right./You're all wrong.

Repeat: Ask if anyone else would like to try but do not give him the matches up your sleeve.

Note: A small piece of silver paper in the hidden matchbox can make it sound slightly louder and more realistic – try for yourself.

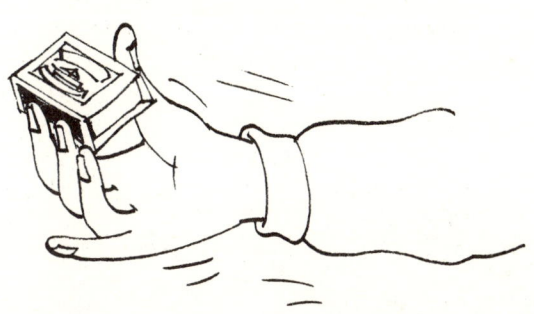

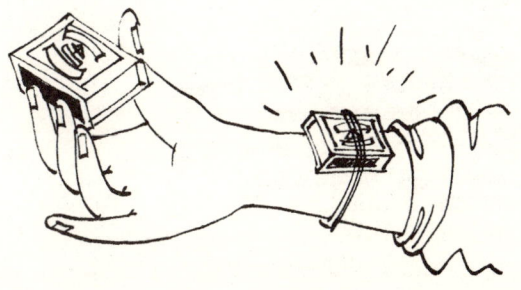

'Which Way Up?'

Magic Trick:	Ask your friends to guess which way up some matchboxes are – they will usually be wrong.
Performance:	A long trick with a large group and some helpers.
Equipment:	Three matchboxes with matches in, some scissors and some sellotape.
Procedure:	This trick is very similar to 'Magic Matchboxes'. Instead of asking 'Which box has matches in it?', you ask 'Which way up is this box?' or 'Is this box the right way up?' and 'Do you think this box is upside-down?' The problem for the audience is that you have carefully prepared the matchboxes as follows:
Preparation:	Take the tray out of a matchbox and empty the matches. Cut the tray in half across its width. Put back half the tray upside-down and half the right way up after joining them together with a small piece of sellotape. Put back the matches in the box making sure that some of the match-heads go one way and some the other. Now if you open one side of the box – the matchbox is the right way up and if you open the other side – the matchbox is upside-down. Repeat this for the other two matchboxes. Your class will be confused and will not be able to remember which way up the matchboxes are if you mix them up well (*and* if you open first one end and then the other end of the matchbox). Practise this carefully and work out what to do and say.

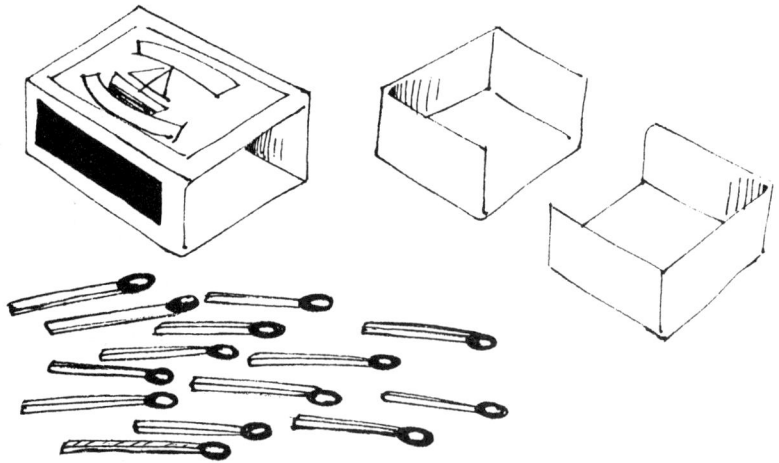

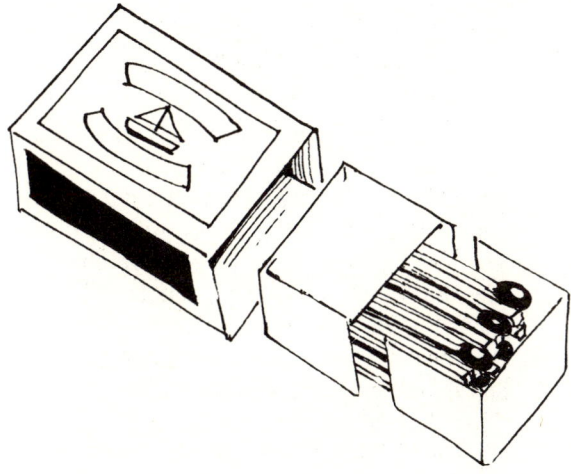

'Right Through the Table!'

Magic Trick:	Make a glass, hidden under a napkin, penetrate the table.
Performance:	Quite a long trick, with a fairly large group sitting down and facing you.
Equipment:	A paper napkin, a glass, a table and chair.
Procedure:	Sit down at the table. Pick up the napkin, and wrap it round the inverted glass – leave the bottom open but twist the top to make a paper shell the same shape as the glass. Next show the audience the glass inside the napkin and then turn it over to put it on the table. At this point, bring the napkin over to the edge of the table nearest you, let the glass slip unnoticed onto your lap and in the same movement place the napkin shell in the centre of the table. Now, pretend to tap the cup carefully on the table-top. In fact, just raise and lower the paper shell and let the hand holding it knock on the table, at the same time tap the glass upwards on the underside of the table (quite hard). Do this three times and on the count of three, quickly smash your fist down hard on top of the paper shell. Then, bend forward and pretend to bring out the glass from under the centre of the table with your other hand. If you follow these instructions carefully, it looks as if the glass passed right through the table.
Preparation:	This trick needs a lot of practice to make it look convincing. Think of suitable things to say to enhance this.

'Found Out!'

Magic Trick:	Tear up a paper handkerchief and make the pieces join together again. The spectators think they have found you out and know how the trick is done – prove them wrong.

EBM–F

Performance:	Quite a long trick with a fairly large group.
Equipment:	Three paper handkerchieves or serviettes.
Preparation:	Before performing this trick screw up two of the handkerchieves into tight balls and conceal them behind the curled fingers of your right hand – not your index finger – keep this free to do other things.
Procedure:	Spread out the third handkerchief on the table with both hands (using the index finger and thumb of your right hand). Then tear it into small pieces. Gather these up and squeeze them into a ball with both hands. At the same time secretly exchange the torn pieces for one of the complete handkerchieves, which are concealed in your right hand.

Say the magic word and spread the fresh handkerchief out on the table. As you do this, drop the other complete handkerchief on the floor, pretending to do this by accident. Hopefully someone will notice this and point it out to the others. Pretend to look 'found-out' and, as you screw up the handkerchief on the table and put it in your pocket together with the torn pieces, make an appropriate exclamation. Apologize profusely to the audience for being so incompetent and then save the day by saying another magic word and opening out the 'indestructible' handkerchief on the table.

The key to this trick lies in practice, good acting and quick thinking.

FOUND OUT!

Section Two: Dealing with Codes

Mindreading: Numbers

UNIT I: Number Tricks

Notes

Language Topics
Talking about numbers and calculations, correcting people.

Level
Performance   – Beginners and above
Reading   – Intermediate
Writing/Tasks   – Beginners to Advanced.

Organization
Another good place to start – classwork with several volunteers or informal large groups.

Speaking Skills
Asking about objects	– What are these? . . .
Talking about quantity	– How many are there?/How old are you?
Correcting people	– No, that's wrong/right.
Talking about actions	– Look I put . . .
Asking people to do calculations	– Now subtract the number of days in a year.

Reading Skills
Verbs	add, believe, choose, count, deduct, demonstrate, do, double, empty, equal, fail, give, halve, indicate, learn, let, make, plus, put, show, speak, subtract, think.
Prepositions	by, in, out, up, with.
Adverbs	quickly, simply.
Adjectives	chosen, even, left, more, odd, right.
Equipment and Related Lexis	blackboard and chalk, calculators, pack of cards, box of matches, paper and pens.

Introduction

In these tricks you manipulate numbers. Most of the tricks here are mindreading tricks – you can guess what numbers people are thinking of.
The first trick ('It Doesn't Add Up!') is a simple manipulation trick which uses words and numbers. The next four tricks ('I Know the Answer', 'One hundred and Fifteen', 'How Old Are You?' and 'The Number You Thought Of') use mathematics to work out a number which someone is thinking of. Ask them to do a sum for you and you can

tell their number and even their age. 'Think of a Number' is a similar mathematical trick but it uses special numbers on prepared cards. The last two tricks ('Numerical Order' and 'Which Card') use codes – either numbers or words so that your assistant can signal to you which number has been chosen.

Tasks for Students

1. Can you think of any other tricks which use words and numbers so that you can guess which number has been chosen?
2. See how many mathematical sums you can find to tell you which number someone is thinking of. You can make this more interesting by guessing someone's shoe-size, collar-size, telephone or house number or the amount of money someone has in his pocket?
3. Ask your audience if they know any mathematical tricks too.
4. If you are very interested in mathematics can you invent any sums of your own?
5. After you have performed a trick, try explaining why (not how) that trick works.
6. More modern number tricks use pocket calculators. If you hold the calculator upside down some of the numbers look like letters try these:
    (a) 07734 – the opposite of 'Goodbye';
    (b) 7734 – the opposite of 'heaven';
    (c) 53045 – the things to put on your feet;
    (d) 71077345 and 7100553 – two large companies.
    Can you work out any more?
7. Try and find some mathematical sums which only work on a pocket calculator, e.g. enter the number 12345679 and ask someone to choose their favourite number and tell you what it is. Mentally multiply the number they tell you by nine and remember the result. Now tell them to multiply the number on the calculator by the number which you tell them – this is the result of your mental arithmetic. For example 12345679 – they choose 5 and tell you – ($5 \times 9 = 45$, remember this) tell them to multiply 12345679 by 45. The answer is 55555555!
8. Can you or your audience write a Magic Number Square – so that the numbers in each row, each column and each diagonal add up to the same answer?

WORKSHEET I: *'It Doesn't Add Up!'*

Magic Trick:	Show how to make six plus five equal to nine.
Performance:	A longer trick with a small group and some volunteers.
Equipment:	A box of matches.

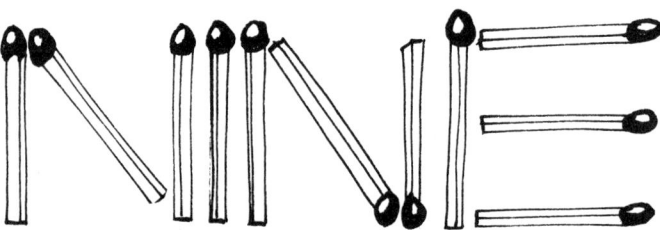

Procedure:	Your students will not believe that you can make six matches plus five matches equal nine. All you do is put all the matches on the table and spell the word NINE in capital letters.
Presentation:	*What to do* *What to say*

What to do

Empty a box of matches onto the table.

Make two piles of matches – one of six matches and one of five.

Let your students try to add the matches together to make nine.

If people fail.

(If someone does it correctly, ask him/her to do another problem.)
Demonstrate the trick.

What to say

What are these? . . .
Yes/No, they are matches.

How many matches are there in this pile? . . .
Yes, there are six matches here.

And in that pile? . . .
Yes, there are five matches.
Now, can anybody add these five to these six matches and make nine?

. . . Here you are. Have a try.
No, that's wrong.
You can't subtract matches./ You can't break them./You can't strike them.

Yes, that's right. Very clever. (Now, can you make four plus five equal ten?)
Look I put the six matches here . . .
And add the five matches like this . . .

You see. Six matches and five matches make the word NINE.

Repeat:	Put the matches back in the box and ask people to show that four matches plus six matches can make FIVE, or four matches plus five matches can make TEN. Then ask them to think of other problems, e.g. ELEVEN, TWELVE, THIRTEEN, etc.

'I Know the Answer'

Magic Trick:	Tell your class to think of a number and do a magic sum. You can tell them their answer before they tell you.
Performance:	A long trick with a large audience and several volunteers.
Equipment:	Paper and pens, blackboard and chalk.
Preparation:	Think of a long even number which is important for you, e.g. your phone number may be 382622.
Presentation:	Ask a volunteer to think of a number, double it and then add an even number which you give to him/her (any even number

will do as long as you remember it). Then ask him/her to halve the result and subtract (take away) the number he/she first thought of. You can then tell him/her his/her answer (this will be half the even number you gave him/her).

Repeat: Repeat the trick with three volunteers all at the same time. They can think of any numbers they like providing you remember the numbers you give to them, you can deal with them all at the same time. Suppose your phone number is 382622 – give 38 to one student, 26 to another and 22 to a third. Their answers will be 19, 13 and 11.

If anyone says you are wrong, give him the piece of chalk and repeat the trick again.

'One Hundred and Fifteen'

Magic Trick:	Work out people's ages and the number they first thought of by asking them to do a sum for you.
Performance:	A long trick with a large audience and any number of volunteers. (People to check the volunteers' work – if you like.)
Equipment:	Some paper and pens.
Procedure:	Give out paper (and pens) to anybody who wants to try this trick. Ask other people to check their work. Tell everyone to think of a number between 1 and 99 but not to tell you, and that after doing a sum *you* will tell *them* what number they thought of. Then tell them to follow these instructions:

1. Tell everyone to write down their own age. ('Please write down your own age'.)
2. Now ask them to double it ($\times 2$).
3. Next tell them to add 5 ($+5$).
4. And multiply the answer by 100 (they can just add two noughts).
5. Divide this number by 2 ($\div 2$)
6. Deduct (subtract or take off) the number of days in a year (-365);
7. Add the number they first thought of;
8. Tell you their answer. ('Tell me your answers, please – one at a time'.)

Now you must write down each person's answer. You must then add 115 to each answer. By looking at your answer you can tell each person the number they first thought of – this will be the two figures on the right of your answer. The two figures (one if he/she is under ten) on the left give the person's age – you can tell them that as well.

Preparation:	Try this for yourself first, then make notes or learn the procedure to make it look more convincing.

```
AGE                          STUDENT A's ANSWER = 1457
DOUBLE IT                         You ADD        115
ADD 5                            YOUR  TOTAL    1572
MULTIPLY BY 100
DIVIDE BY 2                   SO STUDENT A IS 15 YEARS OLD
DEDUCT NUMBER OF             AND HE THOUGHT OF 72
DAYS IN A YEAR (365)
ADD THE NUMBER
FIRST THOUGHT OF            STUDENT B's ANSWER=2665
                           SO STUDENT B IS 26 YEARS OLD
ANSWER-?                    AND HE THOUGHT OF 65
```

'How Old Are You?'

Magic Trick:	Show the audience a new method for working out someone's age.
Performance:	A long trick with a large group and a volunteer.
Equipment:	Blackboard and chalk.
Presentation:	Tell the audience that you have heard of a new way of calculating someone's age. Ask for a volunteer and then follow these instructions:

1. Ask what size shoes he/she takes and write this on the blackboard;
2. Multiply this number by two and write the answer;
3. Add five to this and write the answer underneath;
4. Multiply this by fifty and again write the answer;
5. Add the magic number (this is 1733 for 1983, 1734 for 1984, 1735 for 1985 and so on);
6. Then subtract the volunteer's year of birth and write the final answer.

The last two numbers on the right show the person's age and the numbers on the left show what size shoes he takes.

Preparation:	Try this for yourself first.

'The Number You Thought Of'

Magic Trick:	Five calculations to tell you the number someone thought of.	
Performance:	A long trick with a large group and some volunteers.	
Equipment:	Pens and paper, blackboard and chalk.	
Presentation:	Ask your students to think of a number and without telling you what it is, do the following sums. Suppose they think of 11, try any of the following:	

1.	Multiply the number by 3	33
	Add 1	34
	Multiply by 3 again	102
	Add the number they thought of	113
	You say the number thought of	11

2.	Square the number	121
	Square the number minus 1	100
	Subtract the second answer from the first	21
	Tell you their total	
	You add 1	22
	You halve the answer	11
	You say number thought of	11

3.	Subtract 1	10
	multiply by 2	20
	Add original number	31
	Tell you their total	
	You add 3	34
	You divide by 3	
	(to the nearest whole number)	11
	You say number thought of	11

4.	Add 1	12
	Multiply by 3	36
	Add 1	37
	Add original number	48
	Tell you their total	
	You subtract 4	44
	You divide by 4	11
	You say number thought of	11

5.	Double it	22
	Add 4	26
	Multiply by 5	130
	Add 12	142
	Multiply by 10	1420
	Tell you their total	

You subtract 320		1100
You say number thought of		11

Ask volunteers to try the sums on paper and then tell you their answers. If you follow the instructions you should be able to tell them the number they thought of. If they disagree with your answer, let someone check their working or write it on the blackboard.

Preparation: Try the sums for yourself. Then try to remember what you have to do for each of the methods, i.e.

1. the number thought of . . . first two digits of their answer;
2. . . . add one and halve;
3. . . . add 3 and divide by 3;
4. . . . subtract 4 and divide by 4;
5. . . . you subtract 320 and give the first two digits.

'Think of a Number'

Magic Trick: Guess which number between one and sixty has been chosen.
Performance: A quick trick that can be repeated with any size group.
Equipment: The six cards shown in the illustration, pencil and paper.
Procedure: Ask someone to think of a number between one and sixty and write it on a piece of paper. Now without telling you the number, ask him/her to look at the six cards and tell you which cards have the number on them. Very quickly you can tell him/her his/her number; simply add up the first number of all the cards which contain his/her number.

Repeat: Repeat this trick with someone else.

Think of a number

1	15	29	43	57
3	17	31	45	59
5	19	33	47	
7	21	35	49	
9	23	37	51	
11	25	39	53	
13	27	41	55	

2	15	30	43	58
3	18	31	46	59
6	19	34	47	
7	22	35	50	
10	23	38	51	
11	26	39	54	
14	27	42	55	

4	15	30	45	60
5	20	31	46	
6	21	36	47	
7	22	37	52	
12	23	38	53	
13	28	39	54	
14	29	44	55	

8	15	30	45	60
9	24	31	46	
10	25	40	47	
11	26	41	56	
12	27	42	57	
13	28	43	58	
14	29	44	59	

16	23	30	53	60
17	24	31	54	
18	25	48	55	
19	26	49	56	
20	27	50	57	
21	28	51	58	
22	29	52	59	

32	39	46	53	60
33	40	47	54	
34	41	48	55	
35	42	49	56	
36	43	50	57	
37	44	51	58	
38	45	52	59	

'Numerical Order'

Magic Trick:	Your assistant identifies the number chosen by the audience from a string of numbers which you call out.
Procedure:	A long trick (if you use more than one number) with a large group and an assistant.
Equipment:	A piece of paper and a pen.
Procedure:	Tell your assistant to go out of the room. Then ask your class to agree on a number between 1 and 100, write it on the paper and put it in someone's pocket. Now call your assistant back in. Call out a string of numbers each time asking "Is it . . . ?", "Is it . . . ?" and so on. When you call out the right number your assistant says "Yes that's the one" and of course he/she is right.
	The secret is that the first number you say tells him/her how many *more* numbers you will say *before* the number he/she has to guess. For example, if you start with 5 he just counts five more numbers and the next one will be the right one.
Preparation:	Practise this well, use any numbers you like but don't speak too fast. Take it in turns to go out of the room.

'Which Card?'

Magic Trick:	Although you have been out of the room you can tell your friends which card they have chosen.
Performance:	A long trick with any size group and an assistant.
Equipment:	A rectangular table and a pack of playing cards – without the jokers.
Procedure:	When you are out of the room, your assistant asks the other students to choose a card for you to guess. He/She puts it face-down on the table, but you can tell which suit it is as he/she has put it nearest to the side of the table previously agreed for that suit (see illustration). You then ask him/her questions about the suit, although you know the answers. From his/her replies to these questions you can work out which card it is in the suit, e.g. if you know the card is a club (from its position on the table):

You say:	It's a black card, isn't it?
He/She says:	Yes (if the card is a 2, 3 or 4).
	Right (if the card is a 5, 6 or 7).
	Correct (if the card is an 8, 9 or 10).
	That's right (if the card is a Jack, Queen, King or Ace).
Then you say:	I think it's a club, isn't it?
And he/she says:	Yes (if the card is the first in the set above).

Right (if the card is second in the set above).

Correct (if the card is third in the set above).

That's right (if the card is fourth in the set above).

Illustration: In the example in the picture, the position indicates a Club; 'That's right' indicates Jack, Queen, King or Ace; and 'That's right' again indicates the fourth one, i.e. the Ace so the card is the Ace of Clubs.

Preparation: Be sure to practise this with your assistant. You can use this system for other numbers too.

WHICH CARD?

If practical, other people standing around watching.

UNIT J: Money Tricks

Notes

Language Topics
Talking about value; predictions.

Level

Performance	– Beginners
Reading	– Intermediate
Writing/Tasks	– Beginners to Advanced.

Organization
Large informal groups (but 'Odd or Even' – small group). 'Prediction' requires some reading.

Speaking Skills

Borrowing money	– Has anyone got any loose change?
Receiving things	– Thank you . . .
Distributing things	– Here's one for you.
Giving instructions	– Good . . .
Contradicting	– No, it's even.
Predictions	– I think you will choose.

Reading Skills

Verbs	borrow, call, choose, drop, fail, give, go, hide, hold, lend, point, pretend, put, show, stand, surprise, take, tell.
Prepositions	for, from, in, next, off, on, over, too, under, with.
Adverbs	hard.
Adjectives	different, even, loose, odd, spare, sticky.
Equipment and Related Lexis	card, coins and bank-notes, a cup with a handle, envelope.

Introduction

If you enjoy number tricks you will probably enjoy these tricks too. There are many money tricks which use coins as counters (anything small and circular such as buttons would do instead) but the tricks here all involve the value of money.

'Loose Change' is a location trick where your assistant signals the value of a coin hidden under a cup. 'Odd or Even' is a trick which involves the number of the coins as well as their value. 'Prediction' is a trick which involves careful preparation and hidden objects to tell you which amount of money someone is going to choose.

Tasks for Students

1. If you are very interested in money (we all are, aren't we?) make a list of all the tricks in this book which use coins or bank-notes.
2. Can you adapt any other tricks so that you can use money with them?
3. If you are less interested in money can you use the ideas in this section to invent tricks which use other objects instead of money?

WORKSHEET J: *'Loose Change'*

Magic Trick: Guess which coin is hidden under a cup – and be correct!

Performance: A long trick with a fairly large group, an assistant (confederate) and some helpers.

Procedure: Your students will be surprised that you can guess which coin was hidden under the cup when you were out of the room. The secret is that your assistant points the handle of the cup in a different direction for each coin.

Preparation: Decide with your assistant which coin you are going to use and the position of the cup handle for each coin. Practise in private. Have all the different coins in your pocket in case your students have no money.

Presentation:

What to do

Hold out the cup.

What to say

> I need some money for this trick. Has anybody got any loose change (coins)? Look and see, please.

Choose different coins from different people; each time hold out the cup to them.

> Good. A 1p. Please put it in my cup. And a ½p . . . thank you. I'll have a 5p from you; thanks (etc.). A 50p from you . . . thank you very much.

If any of the coins are missing:

> And I think I'll put in a 10p . . . there, that's enough. Please put away your money.

Give back the coins to (different) people, and give the cup to your assistant.

> O.K. Here's a 5p for you . . . a 10p for you . . . a 1p for you (etc.). And you have the cup.

Tell them the instructions.

> Now I am going out of the room. When I am outside decide which coin to hide, put it on the table and cover it with the cup. Then, will someone tell me to come back in.

Go outside. A coin is chosen and put on the table. Your assistant puts the cup on it (as agreed).

When someone calls you, come back in. Stand at the same side of the table and pretend to look through the cup.

Wave your hands over the cup.

> Now, you must all think very hard about the coin so that I can look through the cup . . . no, harder than that. I can't see anything. Ah, now it's becoming clearer. Good. It's a . . . Am I right?

Repeat: Ask your assistant to give back the coins to their owners. Then start again from the beginning choosing different people where possible, but with the same assistant.

'Odd or Even?'

Magic Trick:	Put some coins in each hand and ask a volunteer whether the total is odd or even – whatever he says you can contradict him/her (tell him/her he/she is wrong).
Performance:	A quick trick with a small group and two volunteers.
Equipment:	Some coins borrowed from the audience (some spare ones in your pocket – just in case.)
Preparation:	For this trick you must choose an odd number of coins which have an even value, e.g. six 1p coins and one 2p coin. Then

you must drop an odd value coin so that you have an even number of coins which have an odd value, e.g. five 1p coins and one 2p coin. Work this out first and have some spare coins in your pocket – just in case.

Presentation: Borrow an odd number of coins which have an even value from the audience (see above). Put some coins in each hand and ask a volunteer if the total is odd or even.   If he/she says odd show him/her that the total (value) is even. If he/she says even, show him/her that the total (number) is odd. Repeat this with someone else.

Now drop a coin with an odd value and repeat the trick – you can't fail if you are careful.

'Prediction'

Magic Trick: Correctly predict what someone is going to choose – a £5 note, a £1 note or a 50p piece.

Performance: A quick trick with a large or small group and a volunteer.

Equipment: A large envelope, a post-card to fit the envelope, a 50p piece (or any large coin) and a small, sticky label.

Procedure: Ask people to lend you some money – two bank-notes such as a £1 note and a £5 note. Put the notes next to each other on the table and put your large coin next to them. Then take the envelope out of your pocket and put it address-side down next to the coin. Tell someone to think hard and choose either of the two notes or the coin. Tell the audience you are sure you know already what he is going to choose. When he has decided, tell him to cover the one he chose with the envelope.

If he chooses the £5 note – turn the envelope over as you have already written 'I predict (think) you will choose the £5 note' on the address side.

If he chooses the £1 note – open the envelope and take out the post-card, as you have already written 'I predict (think) you will choose the £1 note' on the post card.

If he chooses the large coin – take off the envelope and turn the coin upside-down, as you have already written 'I predict (think) you will choose the coin' on the sticky label which is stuck on the coin.

Preparation: Write out the messages and practise it first – you can't be wrong, but you can't repeat the trick either.

Mindreading: Word Tricks

UNIT K: Spelling Tricks

Notes

Language Topics
Talking about spelling, giving instructions, checking.

Level
Performance	– Beginners and above
Reading	– Intermediate
Writing/Tasks	– Beginners to Advanced.

Organization
Informal group work; 'First Word Counts' is more difficult to perform.

Speaking Skills
Naming objects	– What's this . . . ?
Giving spelling	– Here's the word.
Giving instructions	– Please write down . . .
Checking	– Have you done that?
Asking questions	– Do/Can/What/Which . . . ?

Reading Skills
Verbs	ask, bang, continue, cut, draw, finish, know, learn, leave, make, pause, put, say, shout, tap, think, work, write.
Prepositions	at, for, next, of, out, to.
Adverbs	exactly, hard.
Adjectives	alternate, appropriate, big, chosen, interesting, next, numbers (Ordinal and Cardinal).
Equipment and Related Lexis	cards, small objects (ashtray, fork, handkerchief, matchbox, paperclips, pen, pencil, photograph, screwdriver, spoon), magazine pictures, metre rule, ruler, tray.

Introduction

Words, like numbers, are codes which we all use to tell each other about the world. A magician can also use these codes to help him perform magic tricks.

Word tricks are all mindreading tricks. You should always tell the audience that you are going to 'read' someone's mind and then, while you are doing the trick, ask the volunteer to concentrate very hard on the word, object or name which he/she has chosen. This has several advantages:

1. It gives the volunteer something to concentrate on and stops him/her thinking about what you are doing and how the trick is done.
2. It gives the rest of the audience someone else to look at, besides the magician so that they enjoy the trick more. This diverts their attention and they begin to wonder whether you can really 'read' the volunteer's mind.
3. If the trick goes wrong you can blame the volunteer for not thinking hard enough. If the trick is going well, and the magician is enjoying him/herself and wants the trick to go on even longer, he/she can ask the volunteer to think harder: 'No, think much harder! You're not concentrating nearly enough!'

In the first three tricks ('Magic Taps', 'Tap the Picture' and 'Tap the Hole') the number of letters in the word which the volunteer is thinking of enables you to guess this word correctly. Word triangles (see 'Tap the Picture') will help you to choose words to use and learn their spellings so that you can work out the number of letters order. This is the order which you use when you tap the words, pictures or objects.

The last two tricks use speaking and listening as well as spelling. In 'First Word Counts' the number of letters in the first word you say to your assistant tell him/her which object has been chosen. 'Vowels and Consonants' uses the first letter of the first word in each sentence that you say to spell out words to your assistant.

Tasks for Students

Think of some more spelling tricks or use the same tricks with different words.
1. Try using words that are often found together such as the drinks list in 'Tap the Hole' (destinations of international flights may work well).
2. Try guessing people's middle names or home town for tricks like 'Vowels and Consonants'.
3. Can you or your audience write out a Magic Word Square – a number of letters arranged in a square which reads the same across as it does down?
4. Try asking your audience if they can do some Letter Ladders like this: Can you change dog into hat in five moves – each time changing only one letter but writing a complete word?

		Clues
Answer:	Dog	
	Dig	What you do in the garden.
	Big	The opposite of small.
	Bit	Not much.
	Bat	You use this in cricket.
	Hat	

5. Ask your audience some spelling jokes as well, such as this one:
   What is the longest word in the English language?
   Answer: Smiles (because there is a mile between the first and last letters).
6. Try and write a worksheet or text for a new spelling trick.

WORKSHEET K: *'Magic Taps'*

Magic Trick: You tap an object each time your student writes down a letter of the object he has chosen. When he has finished writing its

EBM-G

name you can tell him what he has chosen as you are tapping that object.

Performance: A long trick with quite a large group and a volunteer.

Equipment: A tray with these objects on (and a name-card with the word written on for each object): ashtray, fork, handkerchief, matchbox, paperclip, pen, pencil, photograph, screwdriver, spoon; a ruler for you to tap the objects with and a piece of paper and a pen for the volunteer to write out the name of the object he/she has chosen.

Procedure: Ask a student to think of one of the objects on the tray. Ask him/her to write down the first letter of its name and at the same time you tap an object. Then tap another object and tell him/her to write down another letter. Next, tell him/her to write down a letter every time you tap an object and when he/she has finished writing the name of the object to shout: Stop! Now, continue tapping and when he/she has finished writing he/she will see you are tapping the object he/she has chosen.

Preparation: Learn the number of letters in the names of the objects; you must know the number of letters order:

First tap	– any object.
Second tap	– any object.
Third tap	– object spelt with three letters (pen).
Fourth tap	– object spelt with four letters (fork) etc. . . .
Twelfth tap	– object spelt with twelve letters (handkerchief).

Presentation:

What to do	*What to say*
Tap each of the objects in any order and ask people what they are. Put the name cards next to the objects.	What's this? . . . Yes, that's right/No, it's a . . .
Now say to someone:	Here's the word. Think very hard about one of the objects but do not tell me which it is. Please write down the first letter of that object's name.
Tap any object and leave the ruler on it.	
	Have you done that? . . . Good, now write down a letter every time I tap an object, and when you have finished shout: Stop!
Tap any other object. Continue tapping the objects in number of letters order. Check he/she has written a letter each time you tap an object.	Write another letter! OK? Yes?/OK?/Have you written a letter?/etc.

When he/she shouts 'Stop' you are tapping the object he/she has written.

(Stop) – Look! You have written . . . Am I right?

Repeat: Start again from the beginning but let someone else write down the letters of the name of the object he/she thinks of.

'Tap the Picture!'

Magic Trick: Work out your own magic tricks similar to 'Magic Taps' (Worksheet K).

Performance: Long tricks with large audiences and one or two volunteers.

Equipment: Any objects or magazine pictures, name-cards (unless you are sure your friends can spell the words), a ruler to tap them and paper and pen to work out a word triangle and learn the number of letters order. A (picture) dictionary too.

Preparation: First put the names of objects in a word triangle, so that you can learn the number of letters in each name. You may not need all the lines, especially at the top; you may need more at the bottom.

Procedure: This trick is the same as 'Magic Taps' but you can use bigger/more interesting objects and even new words that your friends don't know. First write out a word triangle using a picture dictionary. Then draw pictures of the objects or cut up magazines. Work out exactly what you want to do and say just like 'Magic Taps'.

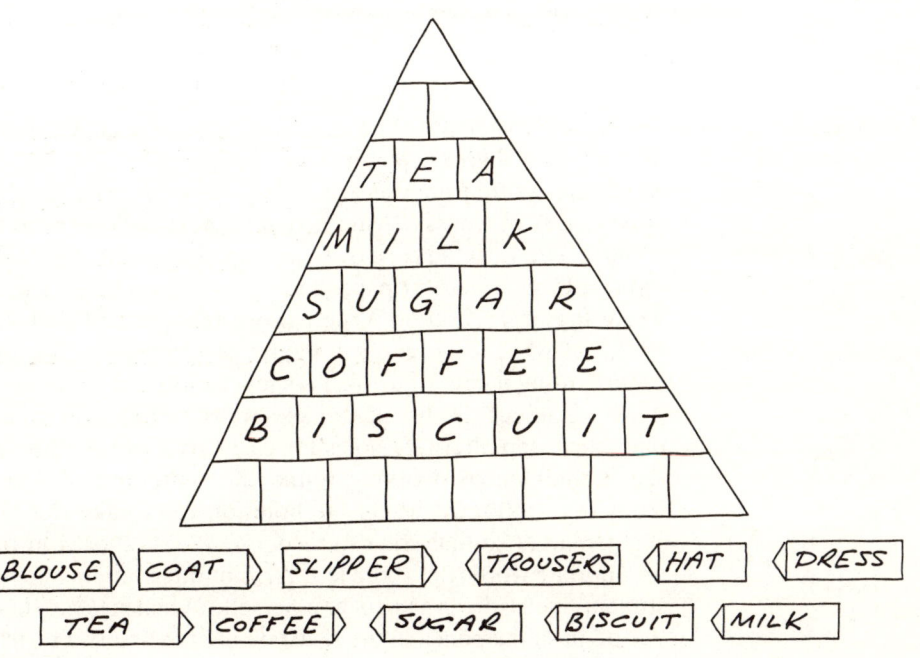

'Tap the Hole'

Magic Trick:	Tap alternate holes for each letter of a word that your student is thinking of and then tell him/her the word he has chosen.
Performance:	A long trick with a large group and a volunteer.
Equipment:	A card with holes in, arranged in a circle, a pen to write the words and to tap the holes and a list of the words written underneath.

TAP THE HOLE

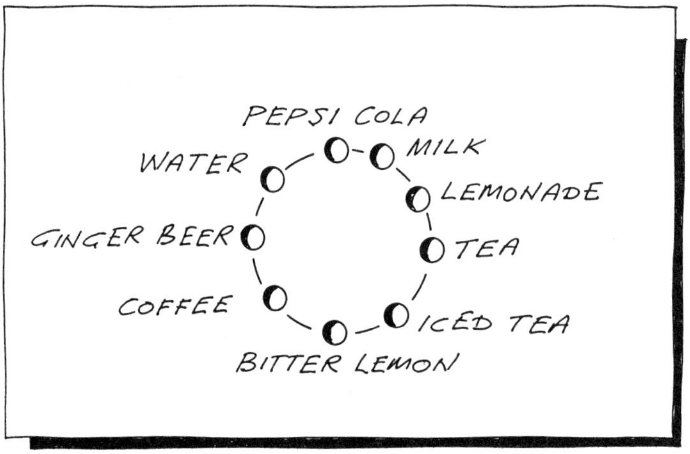

PEPSI COLA

WATER O—O MILK

O LEMONADE

GINGER BEER O

O TEA

COFFEE O

O ICED TEA

BITTER LEMON

Preparation:	This trick is similar to 'Magic Taps' (Worksheet K), but it doesn't have objects/pictures or name-cards. Instead the words are written underneath holes in a card. You need an odd number of words. Write the names next to holes as in the picture. You turn the card over and tap alternate holes. Write the words on a piece of paper too so that your students know which they can choose. Write a word triangle first and then work out what to do and say (as in 'Magic Taps'). The procedure, using names of drinks) is shown above.
Procedure:	Show a student the list of drinks and ask him/her to choose one. Next, tap alternate holes for each letter of the drink he/she is thinking of, working round the circle anti-clockwise. Your third tap must be on the hole for Tea (make this hole slightly larger so that you can recognize it easily) or your own appropriate word (i.e. three letters). Continue tapping as your student spells the word to him/herself. When he/she shouts 'Stop!' push the pencil in the hole you are tapping and turn the card over – it should be the right one!

'First Word Counts!'

Magic Trick:	Your assistant can tell which object you tap is the chosen object from the number of letters in the first word that you say to him/her.
Performance:	A long trick with a large audience and an assistant.
Equipment:	Some large objects, a ruler to tap them and a word triangle as in 'Tap the Picture'.
Procedure:	Your students choose one of a number of objects when your assistant is out of the room. When he/she returns the number of letters in the first word that you say to him/her tells him/her which one it is. If you say 'Do you know what we have chosen?' he/she will know it is the second object you tap as *Do* has two letters.
Preparation:	You and your assistant should write out a word triangle in secret for possible first words. You should also work out the things you should do and say together.

Possible words: *I* hope you can guess what we have chosen – 1
Do you know what we have chosen? – 2
Can you guess what we have chosen? – 3
What have we chosen? – 4
Which object have we chosen? – 5
Decide which object we have chosen! – 6

'Vowels and Consonants'

Magic Trick:	Spell out a word to your assistant by banging a stick on the floor to indicate vowels and using the first letters of sentences you say to him/her for consonants.
Performance:	A long trick with a large group and an assistant.
Equipment:	A metre rule or a long stick.
Procedure:	When your assistant goes out of the room the audience decide on a word for him/her to guess. When he/she returns you spell out the word to him/her using a secret code like this:

(a) The first letter of each sentence you say is the next consonant in the word he/she must guess.
(b) If you bang the floor with your stick the next letter is a vowel:
one bang for A;
two bangs for E;
three bangs for I;
four bangs for O;
five bangs for U.
(You and your assistant must memorize this code.)
(c) You must pause between each sentence or bang.
(d) When you say 'Hey presto!' that is the end of the word.

(e) Remember to tell the audience to think hard about the word so that if you make a mistake it is their fault for not thinking hard enough.

Examples:

*C*ome in. (Pause)	*W*hat are we thinking about? (Pause)
*H*ow are you today. (Pause)	*O*ne bang for A. (Pause)
One bang *A*. (Pause)	*T*ouch the table. (Pause)
Three bangs for *I*. (Pause)	*C*ome here. (Pause)
*R*ight, that's enough. (Pause)	*H*old my hand. (Pause)
Hey presto! What's the word?	Hey presto! What's the word?
This spells *chair*.	This spells *watch*.

Try and think of sensible things to say with all the consonants. If you and your partner get very good you can leave out the bangs and just use the first letter of sentences, but this is much more difficult as you have little time to think.

UNIT L: Speaking and Listening

Notes

Language Topics
Asking about position, describing objects.

Level
Performance   – Good Beginners and above
Reading   – Intermediate
Writing/Tasks   – Beginners to Advanced.

Organization
Large informal groups, concentration on accurate language.

Speaking Skills
Introducing someone – This is my assistant . . .
Making decisions   – Let's choose the table (later in groups).
Alternate questions – What about the . . . ?
                     – Was it that . . . ?
Describing objects   – This is a heavy one.

Reading Skills
Verbs   agree, ask, choose, contain, decide, go, guess, hide, intro-
                     duce, know, look, leave, let, hold, move, point, read, remem-
                     ber, return, say, write.
Prepositions   around, at, behind, onto, out, over, under, with.
Demonstratives   this, that, these, those.
Adjectives   code, heavy, next.
Equipment and   playing-cards, coin, handkerchief, class-list, paper, pencil,
Related Lexis   scarf.

Introduction

You have to say a lot in all these tricks.
You, or your assistant, have to listen carefully for single code words in the first two
tricks ('This and That' and 'What about here?') so that you can find out what has been
chosen. Tricks like these need a lot of practice before they look convincing as you
have to think of other things to say besides the code words.
In the third trick ('Four Legs') you must also think about what the words mean (the
objects they stand for) before you can decide what has been chosen.
The last trick ('By Touch') is a location trick where you name all the cards in a pack.
You must think of interesting things to say to make this convincing.

Tasks for Students

1. Try thinking of some more speaking tricks. You can use any code words you like
   but remember these words must make sense and sound right or your audience will
   easily guess the trick.

2. Can you find or invent any speaking tricks which use an assistant and a telephone?
3. Ask your friends some puzzles like this:
   If it takes ten minutes to fill one bath, how long will it take to fill two baths?
   Answer: Ten minutes (turn the taps on at the same time).
   There are much longer ones like this which use logic. Try and find the one about the man who wants to cross a river in three trips with a hungry wolf, a hungry goat and a cabbage (he can only take two things in the boat with him at one time).
4. Try and find some books about palmistry – reading someone's future by looking at the lines on their hands.
5. Try and write a worksheet or text for a speaking trick.

WORKSHEET L: *'This and That'*

Magic Trick:	Your assistant can guess the chosen object by listening to the words that you say to him/her.
Performance:	A long trick with a large group and an assistant.
Equipment:	The contents of the room and a piece of paper to write the chosen object on.
Procedure:	Your assistant goes out of the room and your students choose any object in the room. When he/she returns, you ask your assistant if you have chosen certain objects, one at a time. He/She knows which it is because you say 'That . . . ' for the chosen object after you have said 'This . . . ' for the one before.
Preparation:	Practise in secret with your assistant. Remember this is nearer to you than that.
Presentation:	*What to do* *What to say*

Introduce your assistant.

> This is . . . He/She will leave the room and when he/she returns try to guess the object we have chosen. OK? Right . . . you can go now.

(Your assistant leaves the room). When he/she has left say:

> What shall we choose? . . . Let's make it simple to start with. Let's choose the table. OK? . . . Good! Call him/her in.(. . .)

When he/she returns say:

> Now we will see what you can do, alright?

Move around the room and point to different objects one at a time and say:

> Did we choose *the* . . . ? (No)
> What about *the* . . . ? (No)
> How about *the* . . . ? (No)
> Was it *that* . . . ? (No)
> How about *this* . . . ? (No)
> Well, was it *that* table? (Yes)

Ask the others:

> Is he/she right? . . .
> Good, out you go again.

Repeat: Remember that 'That . . . ' for the chosen object must follow 'This . . . ' for the one before. You can do this trick several times without anyone guessing the secret. Then try to work out different codes with your assistant.
Possible codes:
– This one and that one;
– Here or there (remember *here* is nearer to you than *there*):
– These and those (for more than one object – *these* are nearer to you than *those*).

'What About Here?'

Magic Trick:	Guess where an object is hidden – when you are blindfolded too.
Performance:	A long trick with a large group, an assistant and a volunteer.
Equipment:	A small object – such as a coin and a scarf for a blindfold.
Procedure:	Your assistant blindfolds you. Then someone else hides the object somewhere in the room. Everyone, but you, knows where it is hidden. Next your assistant goes round the room calling out questions such as 'Is it under this book?', 'Is it behind this cupboard?', 'Is it here?', 'Here?'. Finally he/she points to the place where the coin is hidden and says 'What about here?' you say 'Yes, that's where it is' because of course 'What about here?' is the signal you have agreed upon.
Preparation:	Make sure your assistant knows how to ask lots of questions without saying the code-words too soon.
Repeat:	You can repeat this trick if you and your assistant decide on different code-words for the next time you do it.

'Four Legs'

Magic Tricks:	This is a similar trick to 'This and That' (Worksheet L) and tells you how to develop other magic codes.
Performance:	A long trick with a large group and an assistant.
Equipment:	The contents of a room and a pencil and paper (or class list).
Procedure:	First your assistant leaves the room. Next you write down the names of all the people in the room. Then you write down one or two objects next to each of your students' names. One per-

son chooses the object your assistant must guess when he/she returns. Finally your assistant returns and when objects from the list are read out to him/her he/she chooses the correct object.

The secret is that when you ask him/her if the word was an object with four legs he/she knows that the next object is the chosen one.

For example:

Your questions	Assistant's answers
Did we choose the clock?	No, you didn't.
How about an envelope?	No, you didn't.
Was it a book?	No.
How about the *table*?	No, not the table.
Did we choose a rubber?	Yes, that's what you chose.

You, yourself, must write down something with four legs next to your name if no one else does. You can of course decide on something else instead of four legs, for example: something containing glass. Remember if the trick goes wrong your class weren't thinking hard enough – try again!

'By Touch!'

Magic Trick:	Name all the cards in a pack without looking at them.
Performance:	A long trick with a large group who are facing you.
Equipment:	A pack of playing cards.
Procedure:	Shuffle a pack of playing cards and hold them behind your back. Tell the audience you are going to name all the cards in the pack – not by looking at them but by touch. Hold out the pack in front of you with the cards facing the audience. Then 'feel' the card facing the audience with the fingers of one hand. Then describe the card – 'This card is a heavy one. It's a picture card. It's a king. He is digging. It's the king of spades'. Then put the pack behind your back, turn over the next card without looking and again hold the pack in front of you with the cards facing the audience. Repeat this trick for as long as you like.
Secret:	When you shuffle the pack glance at the bottom card and remember it. When you put the cards behind your back move this card onto the top of the pack with its face upwards. Then hold out the pack to the audience with this card facing the audience and tell them what it is. The audience will think you are holding all the cards in the same way, but as you hold up the pack you can see the new bottom card of the pack. Remember this card so that when you repeat the trick you can tell the audience what the next card is – simply 'by touch'.
Repeat:	Let someone else have a go before you repeat this trick.

UNIT M: Reading and Writing

Notes

Language Topics
Talking about writing, talking about people, guessing.

Level

Performance	– Intermediate
Reading	– Intermediate
Writing/Tasks	– Beginners to Advanced.

Organization
Class group or informal large groups – more difficult tricks such as reading and writing are required.

Speaking Skills

Giving instructions	– Please write . . .
Describing future actions	– I shall write . . .
Encouraging	– No, think really hard . . .
Guessing	– Hmm, let's see . . .
Talking about writing	– Good, it's really neat/clear.

Reading Skills

Verbs	ask, check, choose, concentrate, continue, cut, dislike, empty, finish, give, glance, guess, leave, like, look, memorize, mix, move, put, read, sit, tell, think, write.
Prepositions	at, for, in, inside, on, onto, over.
Adverbs	hard, secretly, slightly.
Adjectives	big, last, marked, next, quiet, sloping, small, upright.
Equipment and Related Lexis	cardboard-box, packet of envelopes, slips of paper, pens, scissors.

Introduction

You have to guess who wrote what for the first two tricks ('Fingertip Reading' and 'Character Reading'). You also have to be able to talk about what they wrote, their handwriting and their character too! The last trick ('Exactly the Same') is a bit of fun! You write the same words on each piece of paper and the words 'Exactly the Same' on another – you can't go wrong with this trick (hopefully).

Tasks for Students

Can you find any more reading and writing tricks?
1. Can you find or invent any tricks which use articles out of newspapers?
2. You can use 'Character Reading' as a speaking trick if you get the audience to draw pictures, instead of writing, for you.

3. Write out a lot of predictions about the future and arrange them in a square. Then work out ways of telling people's future (fortune telling). For instance, throwing several dice or asking volunteers to write down two different numbers – one for the row and one for the column. Now you can read out people's horoscopes.

4. Can you work out any reading and writing tricks using other sections of this book. Here is one that uses numbers too:

Find a book. Open it at page 38 and count down 26 lines from the top. Count eleven words along and write down the word. Then repeat the number trick 'I Know the Answer' (page 104) with three people. Ask someone to use their answers to find the page, line and word given by their answers. Compare this with the word which you wrote down – it should be the same. You can give someone else another number to work out the position of the book on the shelf too. (Prepare this trick very carefully.)

WORKSHEET M: *'Fingertip Reading'*

Magic Trick:	'Read' what is written inside envelopes with your fingertips.
Procedure:	A long trick with a large group and *a secret assistant (confederate)*.
Equipment:	A cardboard box, a packet of envelopes and some pencils and paper.
Procedure:	Your students write short messages on pieces of paper which are put inside envelopes and then dropped in the box. You take out the envelopes one by one and tell the audience each message *before* you take it out of its envelope.
Secret:	The secret is that your assistant has secretly told you his message beforehand and has used an envelope which is marked. Leave his envelope until last.
	You tell the audience his message as you pretend to 'read with your fingertips' the message inside the first envelope which you take out of the box. Next open the first envelope to check it (in fact you read and memorize it) and ask who wrote it – of course your assistant will say he wrote it. Then you pretend that the first message that you read is in the second envelope and so on. Continue doing this but make sure you take your assistant's envelope out last of all.
Preparation:	In secret mark your assistant's envelope and decide on a simple message for him, e.g. 'Meet me at the station'.
Presentation:	*What to do* *What to say*
	Give out the sheets of paper and the envelopes (your assistant must have the marked one)

> Please write a simple message on these pieces of paper. Keep it simple and write clearly as I'm going to read it with my fingertips.

Pause.

When you have finished put your piece of paper in an envelope but don't lick it! Now, put all the envelopes in this box.

When all the envelopes are in the box, look inside it and choose an envelope which is not marked. Tell everyone to concentrate on their message.

First I shall read this envelope with my fingertips. I need your help now. Will everyone put their hands on their foreheads.

Move your fingertips over the first envelope and pretend to 'Read it with your fingertips'. Tell the audience your assistant's message.

Open this envelope to 'Check' the message – in fact just read and memorize it for the next envelope. Ask who wrote it.

Put the message and envelope back into the box immediately and search around for another unmarked envelope. Continue using the message you have just read for the next envelope.

If you get the words slightly wrong, say:

Now think very hard about the message you wrote. No! you must think really hard! That's better. This message says 'Meet me at the station'.

Hmm. Let's see . . . Yes, that's right. Who wrote it? (Assistant puts his hand up) You did? . . . Good, your writing is very clear. Here's another. Think hard. This one says . . . ' Am I right? . . . Good, who wrote it?

Sorry, your writing wasn't clear enough or You weren't thinking hard enough, I'm afraid.

The last envelope you open must be your assistant's but of course you will 'Read' someone else's message.

Finally empty the box onto the table. Ask someone to read out the messages and give them back to their owners.

This is the last one. Think hard . . . This one says ' . . . ' Let's see. Yes, that's right. Who wrote it? You? Good. Please will you read out all the messages and give them back to the people who wrote them.

Repeat: Never repeat this trick immediately with the same group or they will begin to wonder why you always 'read' your assistant's envelope first.

'Character Reading'

Magic Trick:	Read someone's character by looking at their handwriting.
Performance:	A long trick with a large audience and some volunteers sitting next to each other on chairs.
Equipment:	Some sheets of headed notepaper with the name and address of your school on the top. (Or if you can't get any, postcards with the words 'Please write on this side' typed on the top), some pencils or pens and a newspaper.
Preparation:	Before you do this trick take each sheet of paper and put a tiny pencil dot above one of the printed letters (or typed letters) of the heading. Look at the diagram – put the dot over the first letter of the first sheet, the second letter of the second sheet and so on – keep the sheets in order.

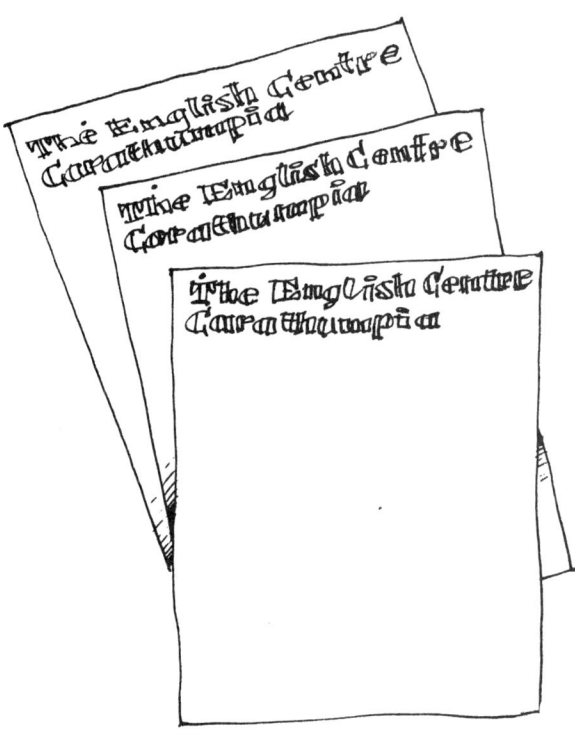

Presentation:	Tell the audience that you are going to do a psychological experiment and read people's character by looking at their handwriting. Then ask for volunteers. Give out the sheets of paper to the volunteers in order. Ask them to write anything they like on the paper. Sit down and read the newspaper whilst they are doing this. Ask someone else to collect the papers, mix them up and return them to you. Now secretly glance at the pencil dot and work out whose writing it is. You can now

talk about the character of the person who wrote it. First read it out. Then talk about the person's handwriting and say whether you think it's a man or a woman. Is the handwriting untidy or neat? Look at the shape of the letters and guess the person's age. Say if the writing is upright or sloping and guess the sorts of things they like to do in their spare time. See if they cross their t's and dot their i's and talk about their character and things you know they like and dislike. Continue like this for some time – guess where they live, what car they have and whether they come from a small or big family and so on. Finally guess who wrote it and give the paper back.

Note: If you want you can tell people to write a letter without signing it, or a story.

You can also tell people to write 'Associations' – the first thing that comes into their head when you read out some words. If you do either of these you can talk about what the person wrote as well as their handwriting.

You can make the trick appear more like psychology and less like magic if you don't say who wrote it, but ask instead.

'Exactly the Same'

Magic Trick: You can tell what someone has written on a piece of paper as you have written exactly the same words on each piece of paper. On another piece of paper you write the words 'exactly the same' – now read on.

Performance: A long trick with a large group and five helpers.

Equipment: Some small pieces of paper and pencils, a box and a pair of scissors.

Procedure: This trick has two parts. You *start part one*, leave it unfinished and go on to part two and *then go back to part one*.

Part one. You yourself *appear* to write down the names of people or objects which your students call out but in fact you write the same name on every piece of paper. Fold up each piece of paper as you are doing this and put it into the box.

Ask a helper to stand up, choose a piece of paper from the box and hold it against his forehead. Ask someone else to cut up the other pieces of paper into very small pieces while the person standing up thinks hard about what's written on the paper. Leave them doing this and go on to part two.

Part two. Ask a third person to write a message on a piece of paper and pass it to someone else. Appear to think hard and then say 'I will write exactly the same on my piece of paper'. Write the words 'exactly the same' on your piece of paper and pass it to someone else. This is really a joke – the first message is read out and then yours. Surprise! Surprise! – you have written exactly the same. If anyone wants to they can check it. Go back to part one.

Part one (continued). Tell everyone to be very quiet and ask your helper to stop cutting. Stare hard, for a long time, at the person standing up who is still holding the piece of paper against his forehead. Then tell him the name on the slip he has taken. Thank him for working hard and tell him to open the paper and read out the name.

Do not repeat this trick with the same group.

Preparation: Practise it very carefully.

Section Three: Dealing with People

UNIT N: Confederates

Notes

Language Topics
Describing people and their characters, talking about numbers and objects.

Level

Performance	– Good Beginners and above
Reading	– Intermediate
Writing/Tasks	– Beginners to Advanced.

Organization
These tricks work well with large informal groups. They are good starters – don't forget to prime your confederate first.

Speaking Skills

Giving instructions	– Will everyone sit . . .
Identifying objects	– Here's the camera/Here's the film.
Asking if something has been done	– Have you taken the photo?
Remembering	– Oh yes, I must develop it first.
Describing processes	– It's coming clearer/It's gone.
Describing people	– It's a man/He's got a beard.

Reading Skills

Verbs	check, choose, clench, come, cough, cover, cross, describe, explain, feel, give, hold, pretend, release, remove, return, roll, scratch, signal, sit, stand, take, tell, think, wave, yawn.
Prepositions	between, from, in, in front of, on, out of, under, up.
Adverbs	carefully, exactly.
Adjectives	chosen, funny, interesting, ordinary, secret.
Equipment and Related Lexis	small ball (rubber, etc.), box, chairs, large handkerchief, paper.

Introduction

These tricks all involve people – a confederate or secret assistant who helps you perform the trick, but who no one knows about (you hope). These tricks all require secrecy, so *no one* must know that you are working together. Make sure that you know exactly what to do first of all. Then, out of class, choose someone who you can really trust and explain exactly what you want him/her to do. If possible, practise the trick at home or out of class with your confederate.

For the first two tricks ('Magic Photography' and 'Hands and Knees') your confeder-

EBM-H

ate signals the chosen person to you. The next trick ('It's in his Face') is a number trick and the last trick ('It Comes and Goes') is a vanishing trick.

Tasks for Students

1. If you get on with your confederate, your tricks work well and no one has realized that he/she is helping you, do some more tricks with the same confederate. Why not keep him/her as long as possible?
2. The simplest confederate tricks are ones where you decide beforehand with your confederate which objects shall be used. Then work out signals (words or actions – such as scratching you ear, coughing, or crossing your legs) to use when different objects have been chosen.
3. Many of the tricks in this book have been written for two people – a magician and an assistant (who everyone knows is helping the magician to do the trick). See if you can make any of these tricks work for a magician and a confederate. You will then be able to do a trick again (after two other people have done it) but this time assure your audience that you have no assistant.
4. Can you work out any more tricks in secret with the help of your confederate?

WORKSHEET N *'Magic Photography'*

Magic Trick:	Develop a magic photograph of someone. As you are doing this describe his/her appearance, his/her habits and his/her character.
Performance:	A long trick with a large group, a volunteer and *a confederate* (secret assistant).
Equipment:	A box, a blank piece of paper and some chairs.
Procedure:	Ask the volunteer to help you take a magic photograph of someone in the audience. Tell him/her that when you go out of the room he/she must stand in front of someone and take their photograph using the box as a camera and the paper as the film. When you come back ask for the photograph and as it 'develops' describe the chosen person and finally give his/her name.
	The secret is that your assistant is sitting exactly in the same way as the chosen person – if he/she crosses his/her legs or scratches his/her arm your assistant does so too.
Preparation:	Practise what you are going to do and stay with your assistant and work out a signal (e.g. yawning three times) in case your assistant has his/her photo taken.
Presentation:	*What to do* *What to say*

Ask everyone to sit in a circle.

Will everyone sit in a circle so that you can see me and I can see you.

Ask for a volunteer.

Now, I need a volunteer to help me with this trick . . . Good. Thank you very much.

Tell him/her what to do.

> When I go out of the room I'd like you to take a magic photograph for me, OK? Here's the camera . . . And here's the film . . . Put the film in the camera.
> It works like any ordinary camera. Just stand in front of someone and take their photo. When I come back, give me the film. Do you understand?

Explain again if necessary.
Leave the room.
Come in again. Pretend to develop the film by waving your hand over it.

> Have you taken the photo? Good, give me the film. There's nothing on this. Oh, yes, I must develop it first.
> Oh, yes. It's coming clearer now.

Glance at your assistant, and begin to describe the person sitting like him. Do not describe the way he is sitting.

> (e.g.) It's a man, I think. He looks about twenty-two years old. He's got fair hair and a beard – No, it's a moustache. Am I right so far?

> He works hard but argues sometimes. He's wearing a blue shirt. It's John, isn't it?

Repeat:	Do the trick again but let someone else take the photo. You can make the description more interesting by talking about the person's character or (if you know him well) what he does at the weekend. It can be quite funny.
Note:	Good for describing people and practise of the present tense.

'Hands and Knees'

Magic Trick:	Your confederate signals which person has been chosen by the number of fingers he puts on his knees.
Performance:	A long trick with a large group, and *a confederate*.
Equipment:	Twelve chairs in a circle (including one for you and one for your confederate).
Procedure:	When you are not in the room, your students choose one person from the group. When you return you can guess who it is. This is easy as one person in the group is your assistant and the number of fingers he puts on his knee tells you where the chosen person is sitting.

Preparation:	Practise these secret signals with your assistant.
	His *right hand* on his knee tells you the chosen person is on his *right*.
	His *left hand* on his knee tells you the chosen person is on his *left*.
	His *thumb* only means the person *next to him*.
	His *thumb and one finger* means the person *next but one to him*, etc.
	His *thumb and four fingers* means the person *next but four to him*.
	If he holds *his hands together it is your assistant himself*.
Note:	If you want to do this trick with a bigger group you will have to work out some more secret signals first.

'It's In His Face!'

Magic Trick:	Guess a number which the audience chose.
Performance:	A long trick with a small audience and a confederate.
Equipment:	Nothing.
Procedure:	Ask your students to think of a number between one and ninety-nine, while you are out of the room. When you return you stand in front of each person, in turn, and put the palms of your hands on each side of his face. Tell each person to think very hard about the number. When you have done this with everyone (including your assistant), you are able to tell the audience the number they thought of.
Secret:	The secret is that your assistant signals the number to you by clenching his teeth. With his mouth shut and his teeth together he clenches and releases his teeth once for every ten in the number (i.e. 46 has four tens). Then he coughs, and clenches his teeth again for the units (i.e. 46 has six units). You can feel this with your hands.
Preparation:	Practise this carefully with your assistant and make sure he doesn't go too fast.
Repeat:	Let someone else try and then repeat the trick.

'It Comes and Goes'

Magic Trick:	Your class feel under a handkerchief. First there is a ball, then it disappears, then it comes back again.
Performance:	A longer trick with a fairly small group and *a confederate*.
Equipment:	A small ball, a large handkerchief (some other small objects).
Procedure:	Roll up your right sleeve (if you have one), hold the ball in your right hand and cover your hand with the handkerchief. Ask all your class to feel underneath and check that the ball is still there. When the last one has checked, quickly pull off the handkerchief – abracadabra! The ball is not in your hand.

Now, put the handkerchief back over your hand and let them all check that the ball is not there. Remove the handkerchief again and – abracadabra! There is the ball in your hand again. The secret is that your assistant is the last to check. The first time he does this he takes the ball away and the second time he puts it back again.

Preparation: Practise the trick carefully with your assistant and work out exactly what to say.

Repeat: You can make other small objects disappear and return, e.g. an eraser, a pencil-sharpener or a ring.

UNIT O: Trick Instructions

Notes

Language Topics
Precise talking, listening and actions.

Level

Performance	– Beginners and above
Reading	– Intermediate
Writing/Tasks	– Beginners to Advanced.

Organization
Any informal groups, work well at any time (stand-by).

Speaking Skills

Putting out equipment	– What are these?
Talking about future actions	– I'm going to show you a trick.
Warning	– once and only once . . .
Reminding	– Now remember the rules.
Giving instructions	– Take two glasses and reverse them both.
Asking for volunteers	– Would anyone else like to try?

Reading Skills

Verbs	be able, break, check, copy, cover, drink, encourage, explain, hold, laugh, leave, make, measure, move, pick, pour, pretend, pull, push, put, (re)arrange, remove, re-set, reverse, sit, shake, stand, suck, talk, take, tell, think, touch, try, watch, write.
Prepositions	across, at, down, from, in, off, on, out, under, up.
Adverbs	carefully, hard, simply.
Adjectives	alternate, confused, empty, equidistant, exhausted, full, middle, mysterious, numbers (Cardinal).
Equipment and Related Lexis	book, box, a lot of coins (two sizes), six glasses, news-paper, table, rubber tube, water.

Introduction

These tricks use people too, but the audience rather than assistants or confederates. They work because the audience are expecting you to perform a magic trick so they do not listen closely enough to your exact words but read other things into what you say (i.e. expecting you to do a movement or construction trick). Because of this, do not perform too many trick instructions one after another as the audience will get bored, or work out how to do them too easily. Instead do them occasionally to surprise your audience and keep the atmosphere light-hearted.

There are many tricks in this unit. They complement earlier tricks in this book. The first tricks all use glasses and others use coins, but you can use other objects too. Just choose a trick that you fancy and tell the audience what to do. Give them a lot of time to try the tricks and then perform it quickly and neatly. (The first trick 'Upside-down' is unusual as you do the trick for them first and then ask them to copy what you have just done.) After you have finished the trick you may have to explain to the audience what you have just done and tell them that you did not break the rules – be sure to tell them in English.

Tasks for Students

1. Are there any trick instructions in your own language that will also work in English?
2. Here's a trick: can you work out how to push a fork through an ordinary finger-ring? Think about it! (Then ask someone else to try.)
3. Can you think of any trick instructions where you have to draw things. Try this: draw four pens for nine sheep so that there is an odd number of sheep in each pen. *Answer*:

Other drawing tricks use dots – you have to join (or separate) the dots using straight lines, without taking your pen off the paper and without going over a line again. Can you find any more?

4. Try some (trick instruction) jokes too. Here's one:
   What will go up a drainpipe down, but not down a drainpipe up?
   Answer: an umbrella.

WORKSHEET O: *'Upside-Down'*

Magic Trick:	Arrange some glasses on the table and tell people to copy what you do. They won't be able to as you have slightly rearranged the glasses for them.
Performance:	A long trick with any size group and some volunteers.
Equipment:	Three drinking glasses and a table.
Procedure:	Put three glasses on the table as in Figure 1. Tell your class they must make three moves – moving two glasses at a time and end up with all the glasses down. Show them how to do it once and *once only*. Quickly reverse glasses two and three, then one and three and finally two and three – all the glasses will be mouth down. Re-set the glasses on the table but this time as in Figure 2. Ask someone to copy your movements –

three moves, moving two glasses at a time. No one will be able to do it as long as you always re-set the glasses as in Figure 2.

Preparation: Practise it in secret with a student and write down a list of things to say when people ask you to repeat the trick, e.g. 'Remember I said I'd only show you once'.

Presentation:

What to do	*What to say*
Put the glasses on the table as in Figure 1 and check people know what they're called.	What are these? . . . (Yes, that's right.) They're glasses – drinking glasses.
Explain that you are going to show them a trick once and tell them the rules. Remind them to watch carefully.	I am going to show you a trick once and once only. These are the rules* – You must make three moves, each time moving two glasses at a time and end up with all the glasses upside-down. Remember watch very carefully. I will only do it once.
Talk them through the trick. (a) hold glasses 2 and 3; (b) reverse glasses 2 and 3; (c) reverse glasses 1 and 3; (d) reverse glasses 2 and 3; (e) look at the glasses.	Take two glasses and turn them upside-down. One! Two! Three!
Re-set the glasses as in Figure 2 and remind them of the rules. Ask someone to try, but only give him one chance.	Now all of them are upside-down. Remember I will not show you again. Three moves, two glasses at a time.
Talk him through the trick.	OK. Who watched carefully . . . Would you like to try?
Explain the rules again if he breaks them. When he has made three moves:	Take two glasses and reverse them both . . . One! . . . Two! . . . Three! No, remember the rules.*
Re-set the glasses and let other people try. Do not repeat the trick yourself until they are really exhausted and confused.	Sorry, you must watch more carefully. You can only make three moves. Would anyone else like to try? Sorry, that's another of the rules. I cannot repeat the trick.

Re-set the glasses for your-self.

Oh, all right. I'll show you once more.
Now watch more carefully this time!

UPSIDE DOWN

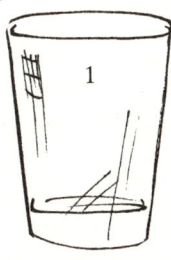 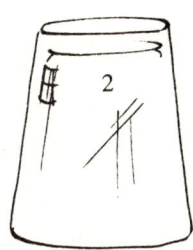 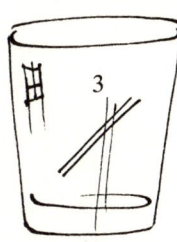

Figure 1

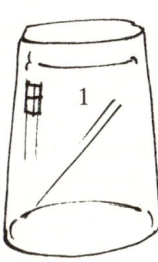  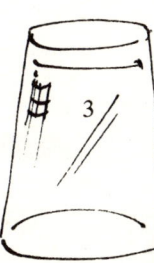

Figure 2

'Only One Glass'

Magic Trick:	Rearrange five drinking glasses so that they are alternately full and empty but touch only one glass.
Performance:	A quick trick with a large group and some volunteers.
Equipment:	Two empty glasses and three full ones.
Preparation:	Fill the glasses first.

Procedure: Arrange the five glasses in a row so that the middle three are full of water. Tell your class that you can alter the row so that the glasses are alternately full and empty, but that you will only touch one glass. Ask them to try and when they give up, pick up the middle one, drink all the water in it and put the glass back in the middle again. The row is now alternately full and empty, yet you have only touched one glass!

'Without Drinking It!'

Magic Trick:	Arrange six drinking glasses so that they are alternately full and empty but only touch one glass.
Procedure:	A quick trick with a large group.
Equipment:	Three glasses full of water and three empty ones.
Preparation:	Fill the glasses first.
Procedure:	Arrange the six glasses on the table so that the first three are full of water. Ask your class if they can move only one glass and end up with the glasses alternately full and empty. Also they must not drink the water. Let them try for a few minutes and then show them how to do the trick. The solution: empty the second glass into the fifth glass and put the second glass back where it came from. Then leave the room quickly!

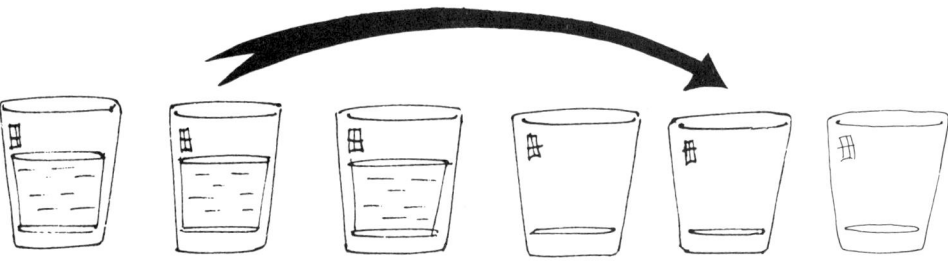

'Watch Me Drink It'

Magic Trick:	Drink a glass of water covered by a box, without touching the box!
Procedure:	A quick trick with a large group.
Equipment:	A box, a table, a glass, a jug of water and a rubber tube.
Procedure:	Pour out a glass of water on the table and put the box on top of it. Now tell your class that you can drink the water without removing the box. If they don't believe you, pull the rubber tube out of your pocket and lie on the ground under the table. Hold one end up to the underside of the table (under the box) and put the other end in your mouth. Now pretend to drink the water through the table by sucking hard on the tube – make a lot of noise when you do this. Now stand up, smile at your audience and point at the box. Eventually they will remove the box to check – immediately you pick up the glass and drink the water without removing the box yourself.
Preparation:	Practise this in secret with a student.

'Pick It Up!'

Magic Trick:	Pick up a coin from under a book – without touching the book!
Procedure:	A quick trick with a large group and a volunteer.
Equipment:	A coin and a large book.
Procedure:	Put the coin on the table and ask a volunteer to cover it with the book. Now, tell everyone that you are going to pick up the coin without touching the book. Wave your hands over the book in a mysterious way and say the magic word – abracadabra! Now ask the volunteer to look under the book. As he does this, immediately pick up the coin and tell everyone that you picked up the coin without moving the book.
Preparation:	Practise the trick first. Try to choose a volunteer who doesn't get angry easily.
Repeat:	At a later date try the trick again using different objects to see if anyone has remembered the trick.

'Shake It Off!'

Magic Trick	Press a coin onto somebody's forehead and then tell them to shake it off. In fact the coin is no longer there.
Performance:	A longer trick, a large group and a volunteer.
Equipment:	A chair facing the audience and a coin from your own pocket.
Procedure:	Ask the volunteer to sit on his/her own hands and face the audience. Take out the coin and show it to the audience but do not let the volunteer see it. Tell the audience that you are going to stick the coin onto the volunteer's forehead and that he/she can keep it, if he/she guesses what it is. Next, press the coin onto his/her forehead, but as you lift your hand up and away, take the coin with it in the palm of your hand.
	The volunteer now thinks he/she has a coin stuck on his/her forehead but everyone can see that he/she hasn't. Remind him/her that he/she must remain sitting on his/her hands and must not try to touch the coin. Then:

1. Tell him/her to guess what the coin is . . . until he/she gets it right;
2. Now tell him/her that if he/she shakes it on the floor he/she can have it but, he/she must not use his/her hands.
3. Encourage the audience to join in if you can.

Preparation:	You can only do this trick once with one group, so practise the actions first and make sure you know what to say. Try to think of other things to say besides 'Shake it off'. Choose your volunteer carefully – someone who doesn't mind being laughed at!

'Farthest Apart'

Magic Trick:	Show that your class can't tell which of three coins are farthest apart.
Performance:	A quick trick with a small group.
Equipment:	Three coins and a ruler.
Procedure:	This is a very simple trick. Place three coins on the table and let your friends see you using the ruler to make sure that the one in the middle is not equidistant from the two outside coins. Then ask them which two coins are farthest apart, as in the illustration. They will probably say the middle one and the one on the right or left as appropriate. Let them measure it with the ruler and then move the middle one into the exact centre and ask them again. Finally tell them they are wrong as the two end coins are farthest apart – ask them to measure that too.

FARTHEST APART

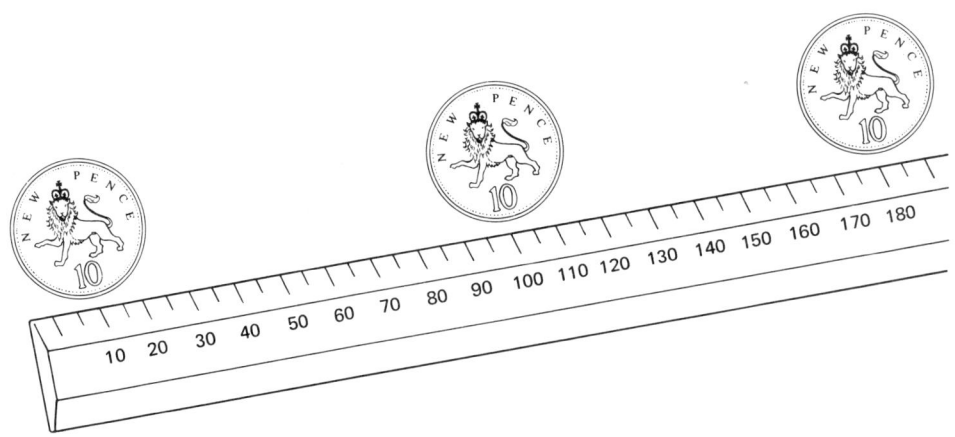

'The Magic Newspaper'

Magic Trick:	Stand on a newspaper in such a way that it will be impossible for your partner (who is standing on the same sheet of newspaper) to touch you.
Performance:	A quick trick with a large group, some volunteers in pairs and a volunteer to help you.
Equipment:	Some double sheets from a newspaper (one for each pair) and a room with a door!
Procedure:	Put a large sheet of newspaper on the floor and ask one person to stand on it. Now ask someone else to stand on it too, but he/she must stand on it in a way that will make it impossible for

his/her partner to touch him/her – without tearing the paper. Distribute several sheets of paper and repeat the instructions to several pairs. When they give up ask for a volunteer and show everybody how to do it.

Open the door of the room and put the newspaper on the floor half in the room and half out. Tell your partner to stand on the paper outside the room. Finally, close the door and stand on the other half yourself – it is now impossible for your partner to touch you.

Preparation: Work out exactly what to say first.

'Across the Cross'

Magic Trick:	Rearrange six coins.
Performance:	A quick trick with a small group.
Equipment:	Six coins of the same value.
Procedure:	Arrange six coins in the shape of a cross with four coins across and three coins up-and-down (see Figure 1). Ask your class to rearrange the coins to make a cross with four coins up and down and four coins across. Let them try and then show them the solution.
Solution:	Simply take the end coin of the cross and put it on top of the middle one – you end up with a cross with four coins across and four coins up-and-down (Figure 2).

ACROSS THE CROSS

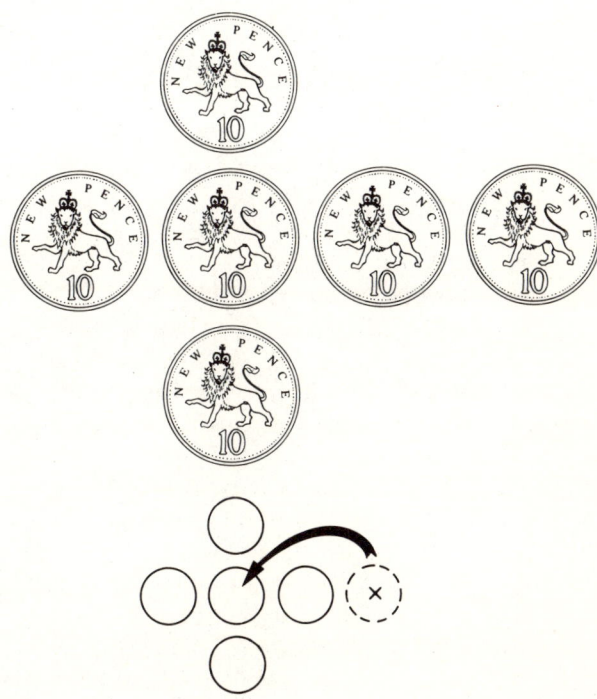

'Alternate Coins'

Magic Trick:	Rearrange twelve coins to make two rows of large coins and two rows of small coins.
Performance:	A quick trick with a small group.
Equipment:	Six large coins and six small coins.
Preparation:	Arrange the coins in four rows of three so that they are alternate i.e., no two similar coins are touching (Figure 1).
Procedure:	Ask the audience to rearrange the coins to make two rows of large coins and two rows of small coins but the rule is: they must only touch one coin. Let them think about it and try. Finally show them the solution.
Solution:	Take the middle coin of the top row and move it round the other coins until it is below the middle coin on the bottom row. Without taking your finger off, push the centre column up one place – you now have two rows of large coins and two rows of small coins but you have only touched one coin.

ALTERNATE COINS

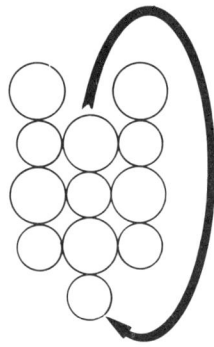

Bibliography

(The following are a few different types of books on Magic)

Written for English-speaking Children

Ladybird, *Tricks and Magic*, Ladybird Books, 1969.
Very good illustrations and tricks. Quite simple language but some new words too.

Collections of Games for Parties

Edmundson, Joseph, *The Best Party Games*, Pan, 1958.
Not many pictures, but written in a clear style. Two chapters on Magic but there are some other tricks in this book which you will have to search for.

Written for Amateur Magicians

Clive, Paul, *Card Tricks without Skill*, Faber, 1968.
A difficult book which introduces a lot of new terminology but starts with a very detailed glossary. A section on tricks of Master magicians too. If you find any books like these (not only about card tricks) written more for professional or serious amateur magicians it may help you to write out your own glossary first.
Gibson, Walter, *Secrets of Great Magicians*, Collins 1967.
A fascinating book with sections on oriental, historical and famous Magic. Good illustrations, very interesting. Easy to understand the Magic but not so easy to do it.
Kaye, Marvin, *The Complete Magician*, Pan, 1977.
A long book full of tricks for many different types of audience – children, adults and 'special' audiences. Very detailed explanations and good advice on how to perform tricks. An introduction on the Magic Circle. Hard work but satisfying.
Lanners, Edi, *Columbus Egg*, Paddington Press, 1976.
Beautiful illustrations, old-fashioned language. Many tricks, games and experiments with objects that you can find easily such as eggs, corks and forks. If you use a book like this you must 'translate' it into modern English before you perform the tricks.
Wright, A., Betteridge, D. and Buckby, M., *Games for Language Learning*, Cambridge University Press, 1979.
Some good tricks for Beginners and other interesting games.

Optical Illusions

Paraquin, Charles H., *Eye Teasers*, Granada Publishing 1979.
Full of interesting pictures; you can amuse yourself too.